'What a helpful book. Positive, poign
helping us see the significant impact
James Lawrence, CPAS, Leadership Princip

'I would highly recommend this book
Rooted in the Bible, Ruth unpacks important aspects of working one-to-one
with young people. It gives the 'why' and the 'how' of doing this and is an
extremely practical book to help young people move forward in their spiritual
journey. I really liked the fact that there is a section on the self-care of the
mentor, which is essential.' Sharon Prior, Director of the PACE Trust

'The Highway Code for mentoring young leaders… essential reading for
transformational relationships!' Alan Charter, Global Children's Forum

'Discipleship will always work best in the context of close, intentional
relationships… *Growing Young Leaders* is a fantastic tool to aid exactly this kind
of life-changing discipleship work. The kind of mentoring that it advocates and
resources isn't easy or fast, but it can produce profound results in young lives
that will echo into eternity.' Martin Saunders, Director, Youthscape's Satellites Event

'I find most adults aren't interested in being a youth leader but are keen to
purposefully invest in one young person… Ruth's book is the best book that
I know of which explains clearly the nuts and bolts of mentoring. She makes
it easy to set up and start a mentoring programme and for you, as a mentor,
to grow in the process. It is so good, it's the one book that I put into the hands
of all the new mentors that we have investing in our young people, and I am
delighted that it has been reprinted. This is essential for youth ministry in the
21st century.' Andy Castle, CEO and founder, Thrive Youth Ministries

'This is a perfect little handbook for anyone considering or already mentoring
young people. Ruth gives us a perfect blend of the theoretical and biblical basis
for mentoring, together with a very practical and insightful guide to all aspects
of mentoring young people, all the while being utterly inspirational! Coming
from an experienced and authentic thinker and practitioner such as Ruth, it's a
must-read for youth work proficionados and newbies alike.'
Helena Kittle, YWAM, England

'This is a brilliant book; Ruth's lived experience of her writing gives her
authenticity and authority. This is a must-read for all youth workers and anyone
who wants to see the church grow.' Rachel Retallick-Cheel, Youth and Support Worker
for The Feast Birmingham

'This isn't so much a book to read and then move on, as it is a tool box to open
and find on every page great advice, tips and suggestions… If you want to
embark on the adventure of mentoring, then get this book!' Ali Campbell,
Youth and Children's Ministry Consultant, The Resource

15 The Chambers, Vineyard
Abingdon OX14 3FE
brf.org.uk

Bible Reading Fellowship is a charity (233280)
and company limited by guarantee (301324),
registered in England and Wales

ISBN 978 1 80039 128 4
First published 2009
Second edition published 2022
10 9 8 7 6 5 4 3 2 1 0
All rights reserved

Acknowledgements
Unless otherwise stated, scripture quotations are taken from The Holy Bible, New
Living Translation, copyright © 1996, 2004, 2007, 2013. Used by permission of
Tyndale House Publishers, Inc., Carol Stream, Illinois 60188. All rights reserved.

Scripture quotations marked NIV are taken from The Holy Bible, New International
Version (Anglicised edition) copyright © 1979, 1984, 2011 by Biblica. Used by
permission of Hodder & Stoughton Publishers, an Hachette UK company. All rights
reserved. 'NIV' is a registered trademark of Biblica. UK trademark number 1448790.

Every effort has been made to trace and contact copyright owners for material
used in this resource. We apologise for any inadvertent omissions or errors, and
would ask those concerned to contact us so that full acknowledgement can be
made in the future.

A catalogue record for this book is available from the British Library

Printed and bound by CPI Group (UK) Ltd, Croydon CR0 4YY

GROWING YOUNG LEADERS

A PRACTICAL GUIDE TO MENTORING TEENS

RUTH HASSALL

For Mum and Dad,
with love and thanks for the strong
foundation of faith you gave me to walk on,
and for your ongoing love and support
in each new season.

Contents

Foreword

I gave my life to Jesus Christ as a ten-year-old growing up in Uganda. The love, patience and advice of those Christian people close to me was vital to my spiritual growth.

Young believers have many pressures, challenges in the faith and temptations in today's society, so it is essential that they have good Christian leaders supporting and pastoring them. When it is applied well, mentoring can be an extremely useful tool in helping teenagers negotiate the dangers and pitfalls of life, as well as providing someone to share in their joys and encouragements. I was very fortunate to have been supported by Bishop Festo Kivengere, Canon Peter Kigozi and Mr Ken Saulez – the latter providing a home for me for five years!

I hope and pray that this book will help release the potential of our young people so that they become even greater disciples of Jesus Christ.

Dr John Sentamu
Former Archbishop of York

Introduction

It's been twelve years since I first wrote *Growing Young Leaders*, and much water has passed under the bridge since then and many things have changed. However, one thing that hasn't changed is my absolute belief in the effectiveness, significance and joy of mentoring young people.

It's been so encouraging to see many churches now offering some sort of mentoring programme for young people and seeing the benefit of it, recognising that while programmes are hugely important in the life of youth ministry, people matter more. It's adults committed to intentionally sharing time, life and the gospel with young people that ultimately make the difference.

I think it's worth highlighting at this point that this book on mentoring is written within a particular context. There are many different approaches to mentoring young people, but the focus of this book is mentoring young people for the leadership roles that they play, whether in church, in school or in their community. Having said that, hopefully the framework and guidelines set out here will be useful and offer support for a wider approach to mentoring.

My prayer, as with the first edition, is that God would breathe life into these words, and that, as a result, the lives of both adults and young people would be transformed for the sake of his kingdom as together we follow his call and leading.

Ruth Hassall

Part I

What do we mean by mentoring?

1

A biblical perspective

The Bible clearly shows us that God's primary method of investing in the emerging generations is through a mentoring relationship.[1]

Mentoring is not a new phenomenon, a fad that the whole world and his wife, including the church, is adopting. It is actually based on one of the oldest models of learning, with its roots way back in the golden era of Greece, many centuries before Christ was born.

Mentor was a character in Homer's *Odyssey*, who in his later years befriended King Odysseus. When Odysseus left to fight the Trojan war, he appointed Mentor to watch over his son, Telemachus, asking him to teach the young man wisdom and prepare him to assume his royal responsibilities one day. Mentor demonstrated many of the key characteristics that are needed by those who instruct young leaders-in-training – wisdom, good character and a commitment to teaching the next generation. So the word 'mentor' was adopted firstly to describe the method of teaching both professional and manual labour skills to the next generation, and, more recently, to define the process of encouraging the growth of a young leader.

Cultural anthropologists tell us that almost every society has 'elders' of some kind. Whether they are tribal chieftains, village heads, clan leaders or family patriarchs and matriarchs, nearly every social unit across history and around the globe includes clearly recognised adult role models or wisdom figures. They are usually older, more experienced, stronger members of the group to whom the younger ones look for a sense of identity.

There are many current ways of defining mentoring, and in chapter 2 we'll look further at some models of mentoring and how they work in practice, but for now it might be helpful to understand the definition that I'm using as I write this book:

Mentoring is a relationship in which one person helps another to grow in their faith and leadership ability by sharing the God-given resources of skills, wisdom, knowledge and experience.

Often, when I talk about this subject in relation to Christian youth ministry, it's not too long before this question is asked: 'Mentoring is all well and good, and obviously a really useful tool… but is it biblical?'

Good point. If you were to look up the word in a Bible concordance, I can pretty much guarantee that you wouldn't find it. Even in the modern paraphrase *The Message*, it only appears three times (Proverbs 5:13; Isaiah 54:13; James 5:10). The word 'mentor', then, isn't a biblical word, but the concept of mentoring is woven right through the Bible, throughout the Old Testament in the lives of the patriarchs and prophets and through the New Testament in the ministry of Jesus and the apostles – as well as in the instructions for the churches in the epistles.

I'd like to take the next few pages to look at some of these relationships, which take different forms. Some of the relationships are quite short-term and are about passing on wisdom and advice; some focus on instructions about hearing and responding to the word of God; some are simply concerned with sharing life together. All of them involve some kind of commitment between two people.

Old Testament

These are just a few of the mentoring relationships that can be found in the Old Testament, and, interestingly, if you follow them through you will often discover that there's a chain developing. As one person has been mentored, he or she goes on to identify and mentor others.

Jethro and Moses

Exodus 18 gives us a brilliant insight into the relationship between Moses and his father-in-law, Jethro. Moses' wife Zipporah and his two sons have been living with Jethro, and, when word reaches them about the amazing things that God has done for the Israelites, Jethro comes to visit Moses along with Zipporah and the boys. While there, Jethro sees what Moses has been facing with all the people of Israel: queues lining up to complain about one thing or another so that the burden has become too much for Moses to carry alone. Instead of just sympathising with him, Jethro takes Moses aside and introduces him to the idea of delegation, giving him wise advice on how to manage such a large group of people without suffering burn-out in the process.

Moses and Joshua

Having received this good advice, Moses recognises that he needs to train up someone who will take on the overall leadership role when he dies. He identifies Joshua, son of Nun, as the person with the potential to do this (Numbers 27:18–23). Joshua had been part of the group sent into Canaan to scout out the land: out of the twelve that went, only he and Caleb had had the confidence and courage to trust God to deliver on his promise of giving them the land even despite massive opposition (Numbers 14:6–9). Moses appoints Joshua to be his assistant and trains him up so that when the time of Moses' death finally comes, Joshua is ready to take on the role of leading the Israelites into the promised land and is recognised by the people as God's chosen leader (Joshua 1:16–17).

Deborah and Barak

Deborah comes on to the scene at a time of war. She was a prophetess and the fourth and only female judge of pre-monarchic Israel; her story is told twice in chapters 4 and 5 of Judges, where we read the account of the victory of Israelite forces led by General Barak.

From the account, we can see that when Deborah calls Barak he is reluctant to go and fight, and with good reason – the enemy army is huge. Barak sets the terms for his participation by insisting that Deborah has to go with him (Judges 4:8). Deborah agrees and proceeds to teach him what it means to go to war trusting in God.

Eli and Samuel

In probably one of the best known stories of the Bible, we have what could be argued is the first recorded example of residential youth work (1 Samuel 3)! Samuel's parents had dedicated him to God, to serve in the shrine at Shiloh, and it was Eli's role as priest to train him in the duties that were involved, but also in how to hear and respond when God speaks. The first time God calls Samuel, the young boy doesn't realise that he is hearing the voice of the Lord, and Eli needs to instruct him about what to say and do when he hears the call again (vv. 7–9).

Elijah and Elisha

Elisha, probably most famous for raising the Shunamite widow's son back to life, is selected by God to be Elijah's successor as prophet, and is appointed by Elijah to be his assistant and disciple (1 Kings 19:16–21). On meeting Elisha, Elijah goes over to him, throws his mantle over Elisha's shoulders, and at once adopts him as a son, teaching him all that is necessary for him to take on the role of prophet. At the end of his mentor's life, Elisha asks for, and receives, a 'double portion' of Elijah's prophetic spirit (2 Kings 2:9–15).

Mordecai and Esther

Esther, in the book of her name, is an orphan who has been adopted by her cousin Mordecai. She is just an ordinary Jewish girl in exile, until one day she finds herself caught up in the Persian king's beauty pageant (Esther 2:8) and God's rescue plan for the Jewish nation. Mordecai supports Esther, challenging and advising her as she approaches the king to help save the Jews from genocide (4:13–14).

New Testament

Jesus

In many ways, Jesus can be held up as the ultimate mentoring model, as his whole ministry was dedicated to investing primarily in the lives of twelve people. In the context of CPAS's *Growing Leaders* course, we call this the Jesus Principle: 'for the sake of many invest in a few'. Jesus understood very clearly that, as mentoring author Robert Clinton puts it, 'more time with less people equals greater impact for the Kingdom'.[2]

As we know, Jesus spent a lot of his time travelling around preaching the good news of the kingdom, healing the sick, casting out demons and getting alongside people who were marginalised, but, as we read through the Gospels, it's staggering to see how regularly he took time out to be with the twelve disciples:

> Jesus' focus was always on relationship and his ministry was in perfect balance: he gathered and spoke to crowds but never allowed their size or adulation to trick him into thinking he had done his work. Rather, while speaking and ministering to the many, he also found a few young men and women to invest in deeply, and with the power of the Holy Spirit, that band of followers turned the world upside down. This generation needs that to happen again.[3]

In Mark 3:14 (NIV) we're told that Jesus 'appointed twelve that they might be with him'. He shared the whole of life with this small group. He wasn't inviting them on a ministry training course; he was inviting them into a life-on-life discipling relationship that would develop them from immature followers to mature, godly leaders.

Barnabas

Barnabas was a man with an incredible ability to spot the potential in others. His real name was Joseph but the apostles nicknamed him Barnabas because it means 'Son of Encouragement' (Acts 4:36). What a great reputation to have! We're also told that he was a man full of faith and the Holy Spirit (11:24). If anyone embodies what it means to be a mentor, it's Barnabas.

Barnabas recognised the potential in Paul when the other believers wanted to keep their distance from him because of his reputation as a persecutor (9:27). He stayed faithful to Paul and was willing to stand by him. However, he wasn't blind to Paul's faults, and, when Paul was unwilling to give John Mark a second chance to participate in ministry, Barnabas challenged him, ending their partnership (15:37–39).

Paul

It's no surprise that Paul went on to mentor others in the same way that Barnabas had mentored him. Most notable among Paul's mentorees are Timothy and Titus, Silas, and Priscilla and Aquila.

On one of his missionary journeys, Paul met Timothy and spotted great potential in this young leader. Paul invited Timothy to travel with him, giving him opportunities to serve and to grow in leadership experience (Acts 16:1–3). The two letters that he wrote to Timothy continued the mentoring relationship even when he couldn't be there in person, giving good advice for the different situations that Timothy was facing. He also encouraged Timothy to continue the mentoring tradition by reaching out to other potential leaders: 'You have heard me teach things that have been confirmed by many reliable witnesses. Now teach these truths to other trustworthy people who will be able to pass them on to others' (2 Timothy 2:2).

As we read the letters that Paul wrote to the churches, we can find further examples of the way he invested in the lives of others:

- He was aware that our love for the young in faith must go further than simply sharing with them the good news: 'We loved you so much that we shared with you not only God's Good News but our own lives, too' (1 Thessalonians 2:8).
- He knew that his life was a great resource in demonstrating what it meant to be a follower of Christ: 'Imitate me, just as I imitate Christ' (1 Corinthians 11:1, NIV).
- He wanted the young leaders to know that what he taught was trustworthy and provided practical skills for the work of mission: 'Keep putting into practice all you learned and received from me' (Philippians 4:9, NIV).

Youth ministry trainer Paul Fenton sums up well Paul's understanding of what young leaders needed from him:

> He knew that when the young in faith stumbled on rocky ground, they would need someone to steady them; when they reached the hilltops, they would need someone to join the celebration; when they faced a crossroads, they would need someone to share in the decision to take the narrow path; when they faced dark valleys of despair, they would need someone to lean on.[4]

Those were not just the needs of young leaders in the early Church; those same needs are present today.

Is this not 'discipleship'?

In previous generations, mentoring, as talked about here, may well have been described as 'discipleship', and I think that discipleship still plays a large part in what we mean by 'mentoring' in the Christian context. This is reflected in the first part of our definition: 'Mentoring is a relationship in which one person helps another to grow in their faith…' Mentoring goes further, however, in that it's also about seeing potential in young people and helping them to identify and grow in their skills and gifts.

As we saw at the beginning of this chapter, mentoring isn't a new phenomenon. This kind of relationship has always been part of the Bible's story, but it seems to me that in recent years we have lost sight of it. Much has been done to improve the way churches provide for young people, recognising that they have distinct learning needs, and so on. But over this last century I think there has been a tendency to become more concerned with education than with spiritual formation – or, if I'm honest, more concerned with entertainment than spiritual formation! We can only begin to fulfil the great commission of Jesus to make disciples of all nations (Matthew 28:19) if we start investing time in the lives of young believers.

When I started working as a youth pastor in a local church, I was desperately looking for the one 'great thing' that would attract and keep young people. When I'd been at the church for about a year, I took some time away to think through the future direction of the youth ministry. I went armed with my Bible and a notebook, ready to hear from God some master plan that would transform the nation, but the only phrase that kept coming to my mind was 'Spend time with them'. I have to admit, it took me a while to realise that this was God's master plan and, in fact, always has been.

As we read through the Bible, we can see that it's there right from the start. Deuteronomy 6:6–7, for example, commands parents and carers to talk about God's laws to their children – not in a classroom but in everyday life. It's as if God says, 'Do you want the next generation to share your values, the values I gave you? Then they'll have to see those values demonstrated in your life so consistently that, no matter what you do, they shine out of you.' Mentoring is not parenting – let's be clear about that – but in some respects it uses the same 'when you are at home and when you are on the road' method that God gave to parents and carers in Deuteronomy 6. The effectiveness of this kind of training is backed up by Proverbs 22:6, where we read, 'Teach your children to choose the right path, and when they are older, they will remain upon it.'

When God wanted to communicate with his people in a definitive way, he didn't create a programme. He sent his Son – Emmanuel, the God who is with us, who invested time in his followers and taught them to be like him. And the new heaven and earth, promised by God at the very end of the Bible, is a picture of a place where God is present with his people, where they see him face to face (Revelation 21:3; 22:4).

In many ways, the whole issue of mentoring isn't really about youth work at all. It is about a way of life, a way that God intended from the start, and a way that Jesus has called us all to follow, as soon as we realise that it is our responsibility to make disciples of all people.

Spiritual formation is never about how many training programmes a church runs or even about the quality of those programmes. It is about the quality of the people with whom young people are interacting, and the overall spiritual and relational quality of the community of faith.

Connie's story

When I was 14 I became a Christian after always having gone to church but never having realised that Jesus wanted to know me or that I could know him too. I was a very insecure girl without any idea of self-worth, who looked for anything or anyone to find identity in. My parents had split up when I was 11 and it had turned my world upside down. When I first felt God, all I could do was cry, and it continued like that for a long time. My youth pastor who became my mentor got alongside me and met up with me every week during my teenage years. She taught me so much about God and encouraged me to keep looking to him. Back then my behaviour had not changed very much but I never felt condemned by her. There were times when I hit rock bottom and my mentor was the person I called on. I feel God brought her into my life to show me love and to cause me to trust when I felt betrayed. With her support I have been able to overcome many things and become more the person and the leader that God created me to be.

Connie's testimony shows us that God didn't create people to be self-sufficient and move through life alone: we need healthy supportive relationships. This is recognised in many areas of life, but in no area is it so crucial as in the development of young leaders, to ensure that they are mentored in a biblical way.

2

Models of mentoring

Our chief want in life is somebody who shall make us do what we can.
Ralph Waldo Emerson

Although the word 'mentoring' is not directly mentioned in the Bible, we've now seen that the concept is a truly biblical one and is, in fact, connected with Jesus' great commission to us to 'make disciples'.

Furthermore, mentoring in the church context is unique because here the mentor does more than just passing on skills. Rather, this is spiritual leadership – a calling to lifestyle and faith formation and an opportunity to plant in the next generation the desire to be disciple makers themselves: leadership consultant John Mallison says, 'It is quite awesome that the mentor as Christ's representative makes disciples who are able to make disciples to teach others also! Producing a Christlike disciple who "can teach others also" is a formidable task.'[1]

The teenage years are such a significant time to be involved in young people's lives. They are a time of growth and development, providing opportunities to help form values and set up a pattern for life. We should remember, though, that mentoring is an intentional relationship: it won't happen by accident. The people involved need to be clear about why they're meeting, and, while there is a large element of friendship involved, it remains a relationship with a purpose.

Mentoring is important because it's a key way of sharing not just information but our whole lives, enabling others to see in action what it means to be a Christian leader and learn from it. As we've noted, this is the relationship Paul had with Timothy. They would have travelled around together and Timothy would have seen Paul in action, preaching and teaching, and would also have been involved with him in setting up new churches. Paul wanted Timothy to remember all that he'd learnt, not just keeping it to himself but passing it on to others who were also involved in leadership.

What's great about mentoring relationships is that they can happen in a number of different contexts. The pattern set out in the Bible seems to be that as we reach out to someone ahead of us who will teach, encourage and inspire us, at the same time we should be stretching out the other hand to someone younger, either in age or in faith. Each one of us has plenty to learn from someone else, and plenty to offer someone coming up behind us.

The mentoring network

At present I am involved in a number of mentoring relationships.

First, I am being mentored myself. My mentor is the person who consistently challenges me professionally, personally and spiritually. They are the person who has permission to ask me difficult questions about my life, and has my commitment to be honest about how things really are. We meet together once a month for about an hour and a half, and I can honestly say that that time is the most significant hour and a half of every month. It gives me the chance to reflect with someone else on the happenings of the previous few weeks, the state of my relationships, things that I think God has been saying to me and where I think he's leading me. I always leave feeling challenged to keep on being the person God has called me to be, encouraged and built up in my identity, and hugely humbled by the gift of time and focus that I have been given.

Second, I am currently mentoring a number of people who are involved in different forms of ministry. I meet with each of them about once a month and we talk about key issues for them, predominantly to do with their work but also about their relationship with God. Although theoretically I am the one giving to them, I always come away feeling encouraged and inspired for my own life and work. It is such a privilege to be able to share in other people's lives, to hear their hopes, dreams and concerns and be part of praying for those issues.

As John Mallison puts it:

> I don't presume to know God's will for them. But it is a privilege to listen carefully to their joys and sorrows, to encourage and support them, to pray with them and for them, and to keep pointing them to Jesus as their reason for living, loving and serving... And in the whole process, I find that God has much to say to me, and that I too am enriched and encouraged.[2]

Thirdly, I meet with two friends on a regular basis. We have a meal together and take some time to read the Bible and pray for each other and for our church.

Fourthly and finally, I'm mentored by people I've never met and am highly unlikely to meet – Christian leaders whose biographies I read. Two such books that have inspired me in different ways are the autobiography of a Christian businesswoman, Carly Fiorina, and the biography of Amy Carmichael, a missionary to India. In her autobiography, Carly Fiorina tells her story of working within the business world and how she developed her leadership skills there; Amy's story of her life and commitment to following God into some really dark places has challenged me enormously. As I have spent time with these women, though not in person, I have learnt so much from them and feel encouraged to grow in my relationship with God and to use my gifts and skills to serve others.

At the moment, then, my mentoring network looks something like this:

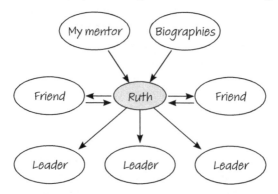

We're all called to be a mentor and to find mentors. The way to become a mentor is to develop a personal list of young people to watch out for. Be intentional in this: deliberately draw closer to someone and look for God-given opportunities to develop a mentoring relationship. And be intentional about finding mentors. Seek out spiritually mature people whom you admire and ask them to help you find a mentor.

Images of mentoring

There are several helpful images that we can use to illustrate the role that a mentor plays in the life of a young person.

- **Coach:** A coach is someone who cheers you on in a race or match, critiques it with you afterwards and provides encouragement and pointers for the way ahead.

- **Guide:** A guide lays out options and choices for you, for the different paths you may want to follow. They point out possible dangers along each path but never tell you exactly what to do. This is important: as tempting as it may be, the mentor's role is not to tell young people what to do but to help them gain the skills to make good decisions for themselves.

- **Sponsor:** In the mentoring context, the sponsor can open doors to people, ideas and opportunities to which the young person might not otherwise have access.

All of these models are equally valid. The key thing is to identify the young leader's particular needs at any point in time. If they need someone to help them develop the skills of leadership, then the 'coach' model will be the dominant model used. In my experience, however, a combination of models is needed, in order to support the young leader fully at each moment in their life.

What mentoring is not

Mentoring is not about being a parent. We need to be aware of this because many young people are looking for a parent figure. It is important to set clear boundaries early on about the nature of the relationship. If this isn't clear, it is likely that the young person you are mentoring will ask more of you than you can appropriately give, and will end up feeling disappointed and let down. We also need to watch our own motives, as the emotional need may well be on our side. If so, it's vital to have someone to whom we can be accountable about how we're handling the mentoring relationship.

Also, a mentor is not a counsellor. As you get to know each other better, your mentoree may well confide in you about more personal areas of difficulty in their life. Again, it's very important to be clear about the boundaries of the relationship, and we must always be ready to point the young person to someone else who is better qualified to help them with such issues.

A mentor is not a buddy, either. Relationship is a fundamental part of mentoring but it's important to be absolutely clear that this isn't a peer friendship. Being an adult friend to a young person is very different from behaving like one of their own buddies.

Finally, a mentor is not simply a teacher. Of course, the hope is that learning will be taking place within the relationship, but the mentor's role is to be much more than a teacher:

> A spiritual teacher explains things to a student; but a mentor shows the student. Jesus taught about prayer publicly, but with his disciples he prayed while they watched, and then he also prayed together with them. So as a mentor, you wouldn't just talk about prayer, you would pray with the student and the student would 'be-with' you while you pray in various settings. Whereas a teacher might describe how to study the Bible, a mentor does a Bible study with a student; the mentor also reacts biblically, without thinking about it, thus showing that the Word has taken root and is not just an abstract concept.[3]

This is very much the approach that Paul took with Timothy. There was a lot of teaching and learning involved, as Paul intended, but it went much further than that. That is why he was able to write to Timothy:

> But you, Timothy, certainly know what I teach, and how I live, and what my purpose in life is. You know my faith, my patience, my love, and my endurance. You know how much persecution and suffering I have endured... You must remain faithful to the things you have been taught. You know they are true, for you know you can trust those who taught you.
>
> 2 TIMOTHY 3:10–11, 14

This teaching didn't happen in a classroom; it happened as the two men shared life together. Paul didn't just teach Timothy facts and useful leadership tips; he embodied what he taught and demonstrated a whole way of life. This, I think, is one of the key aspects of mentoring teenagers. When mentoring other adults, it is highly likely that we won't see them outside the mentoring relationship. For effective mentoring of young people, though, I believe that they need to be able to see the mentor living out their faith, with all that that involves.

What does mentoring involve?

In setting up the mentoring relationship it's helpful to follow these stages:

- Connecting: building an initial relationship, getting to know each other and making sure that both parties want to continue. (We'll talk more about identifying mentorees in part II.)

- Clarifying: asking the questions 'What do we want to gain from our time together? What are our expectations of each other?'

- Continuing: meeting together on a regular basis.

- Evaluating: every few months, taking a step back to evaluate how things are going. Are expectations being met?

- Adjusting: keeping going and making changes or bringing the relationship to a close.

On the subject of how we mentor, an image I find helpful is that of 'pacing'. In his book *Shaping the Spiritual Life of Students*,[4] Richard Dunn tells the story of how he stumbled across this concept. He was out enjoying a walk with his four-year-old son when he realised that he was striding ahead, leaving the child struggling to keep up with him. What he had intended as a side-by-side journey had become, for his son, a frustrating effort not to be left behind.

When he reflected on this, Dunn realised that there were a lot of parallels in discipling and mentoring young people. So often, we run ahead of where they are, or expect a maturity in faith and behaviour that is beyond them at the present time. Sometimes we expect too little of them and they're left to navigate the way ahead on their own. Young people need adults who will let them set the pace and will walk alongside them, encouraging them in their present situation but also helping them look ahead to what is within their reach.

Once the mentoring relationship has been established, the time devoted to it can involve a whole number of different elements, depending on the purpose of the relationship. These different elements can include:

- Reading the Bible together.
- Reflecting on life since the last time you met – how their relationships have been, where they have sensed God prompting them, issues where they have struggled, and so on.
- Reflecting on leadership opportunities that they have had – evaluating lessons learnt, and so on.
- Deciding on a book that you will both read and then discuss together.
- Praying together.
- Setting some goals for the coming weeks and months.
- Offering encouragement.
- Discussing particular issues that they're thinking about or facing.
- Eating a meal together.
- Doing some leadership activity together.
- Celebrating good things that have happened.

There is no one set way of mentoring, and it's good to explore different avenues. If the relationship doesn't seem to click instantly, discuss possible options for your time together that would be useful for developing the mentoree. Your activities may vary from time to time. One week you may want to focus on looking at some Bible passages on leadership, whereas another week you may want to spend time reflecting on a particular event that has happened. The key thing is to have a direction, to know what you are trying to achieve. We'll look at this further in chapter 6.

3

Benefits of mentoring

A lot of people have gone further than they thought they could because someone else thought they could.

Anon

The mentoring process takes time. Is it worth it?

It certainly does take time, but it is very definitely worth it. As I reflect on my time as a youth pastor, I think that by far the most effective and fruitful aspect of my work was setting up a mentoring scheme and being involved in mentoring some young people. As I continue in ministry today, I remain convinced that the most effective use of my time is in mentoring a few individuals.

After my moment of 'revelation' that I needed simply to spend time with young people (see chapter 1), I returned to work determined to put this principle into practice. It wasn't too long, however, before I was tired and disillusioned. The church where I worked was a large town-centre congregation with a good number of children and young people. There was no way I was going to be able to spend time with them all on an individual basis. I'd manage to see each of them only about once a year.

That's when my next 'revelation' moment occurred: I realised that I didn't have to do it on my own. Each Sunday I was surrounded by a wealth of wisdom, experience and lives spent walking with God. There were many people in church who wouldn't necessarily feel able to get involved in 'youth ministry' but would happily commit to meeting with one teenager every couple of weeks.

Although I'd heard about mentoring at this point, I wasn't too sure how it would work. If each of our young people was to have the opportunity to meet with an adult willing to spend time with them, I needed to look further than just among those currently involved in the youth team. To cut a long story short, I went to the church and asked if there were any adults who would be interested in mentoring teenagers, and then went to the youth group to ask if any of them would like to be part of the scheme. (I shall write more in part II about the practicalities of setting up a mentoring scheme.)

The response was phenomenal. I was overwhelmed by the number of the congregation who came forward, and, although a bit dubious at first, an equal number of young people decided that they wanted to take up the offer. So we paired people up and off they went. A number of years later, some of those young people, well into their 20s, were still meeting with the same mentors.

Once the model had been up and running for a little while, we developed it a stage further by asking the young people whether, as they looked at the life of the church, there were any areas where they would like to be involved. Some said they'd like to be in the music group, others wanted to learn how to use the sound system, others were willing to be involved with prayer ministry, others wanted to be in cell group leadership and yet others volunteered for the hospitality team. Rather than setting up a specific 'youth music group' or 'youth prayer ministry team', we matched the young people with adults who were serving in those different ministries. This meant that not only would they be discipled, but they would also be coached in practical areas of ministry.

What were the benefits of this process? Let me share with you the benefits that we saw and continue to see.

1 Intergenerational relationships

The biblical mandate has always been that 'one generation should tell the next the great things of God, so that the upcoming generation can put their trust in him' (Psalm 78:4–7, paraphrased). The problem is the current way in which we 'do church' often doesn't really allow for that to happen. Why not?

Firstly, relationships with younger church members tend to be limited to the few adults who are part of the youth and children's work, whereas the mandate to 'tell the great things of God' was given to the whole of the people of God, not just those with special responsibility for children. It's for those who have children and those who don't, those who like children and those who don't. The responsibility belongs to all of God's people.

Secondly, as mentioned earlier, we often have so little time with children and young people in church that the model tends to be about educating them in a theoretical knowledge of God rather than helping them to grow in relationship with him. This is not meant as a criticism of youth and children's ministry – many, many people are working faithfully week by week with the children and young people in their churches and doing a fantastic job – but the reality is that real, meaningful discipleship can only happen as a mature disciple comes alongside one or two younger in faith.

By drawing others into mentoring in the church where I was youth pastor, we saw bridges being built between the generations. Older members were now not just a collective group of 'old people'; they had names and stories to share, and the young people loved introducing their mentor to their friends. Also, viewing it from the opposite direction, the young people were no longer just a 'rabble' to the older ones; they had names and personal stories, too. I believe that this helped us move on with our aim to be a true community, with genuine relationships between younger and older church members.

2 Tapping into unaccessed wisdom and experience

There are so many people in our churches who have wisdom and experience beyond what we could imagine, yet week by week they go unnoticed. They may not be leaders in the life of the church, but in their everyday working lives they are demonstrating what Christian leadership means.

Some may have served as missionaries for a large part of their lives, and have now returned home for their retirement years. Even their stories may go untold, though, because the stories are not embodied in youthful-looking people.

I am more and more convinced that we don't have to be, in any sense, young and trendy to be involved in youth discipleship and mentoring (especially the older and less trendy I become!). What matters is that we love God, love young people, have a story to share and have ears that will listen.

I really enjoy hearing young people talk about their mentors, introducing their words with the phrase, 'You'll never guess what they've done…'. Mentoring draws in people not usually involved in youth work, allowing them to come forward and share the gifts of wisdom and experience that God has given them. Such gifts are what young people desperately need.

3 Development of strong leadership

I spend a lot of my time working with churches on issues of leadership, and I have yet to discover a church that has the problem of too many leaders. On a broader scale, research is showing that the average age of Anglican ordinands is now 49. We have a real dearth of leaders in the church, yet we are overlooking a key group of people who are ready to be developed in leadership skills. Many of them already hold leadership positions in their schools, sports teams or community groups, yet there are very few people helping them work out what it means to be a Christian leader in those situations.

If we start developing people in leadership at a younger age, it means that they will grow stronger and deeper as leaders. Many of the young people who were part of the mentoring scheme that we initially set up in my church are now in their late teens and early 20s and are playing key leadership roles. They are equipped to do the job, so they are open to learning more – and that has been their default position from an early age.

Sharon Daloz Parks (Associate Director at Whidbey Institute, Seattle) writes, 'Good mentors help to anchor the promise of the future.'1 Young people have leadership skills that need to be used now, in their immature state, if we're to make that investment in the future. But we do this not just for the sake of what's to come; it's about recognising them as kingdom people now, with so much to contribute.

4 Deepening of faith

Recently I was at a conference for young leaders aged 16–25. During one of the breaks I went to have coffee with a number of the young people, to ask them what they thought made a difference to them in their faith. Why was it that they were still committed to God, having left home and gone to university, growing in leadership within and outside the church, while some of their peers, who'd been in the same youth group, had left their faith when they left the youth group?

Their response to my question: they had had a mentor – someone who had met with them on a regular basis to ask them about their lives and challenge them, and to help them put their faith into practice. They were convinced that this was what had made the difference to them. The mentoring relationship took them beyond a commitment to the youth group and led them to a real commitment to a life with God.

In the church where I set up the mentoring scheme, it wasn't only the young people being mentored who grew in faith, either. Many of the mentors would say that taking part in the scheme challenged them in their own faith. Young people are good at asking searching questions and know full well when you're bluffing! I think that this very well reflects the image in Proverbs 27:17 that 'as iron sharpens iron, so a friend sharpens a friend': the process works two ways.

5 An open door for the future

Not all young people are going to reach adulthood with their faith intact. Some will walk away from the church and leave their faith behind for a while. For many young adults who have experienced this, it is the memory of times spent with their mentor that draws them back. Those memories take root and, though ignored for a while, continue to be an influence on them. The likelihood, too, is that their mentor will be the person they come back to, in order to talk things through.

6 An opportunity to give back

One of the most moving aspects of the mentoring scheme, for me, was that many people whose own children had grown up in the church wanted to do for someone else's teenager what other adults had done for theirs. Many were convinced that their children had weathered the teenage years and grown in their faith simply because of the time and love that certain adults invested in them.

It would be easy to read this chapter and think that a mentoring scheme would work only for a big church with a large number of young people. I would argue that the size of your youth group or church really doesn't matter. You may have only two or three young people in your church, but they are individuals with gifts and skills that need developing and relationships with God that need to be nurtured and grown.

It never ceases to amaze me that I can spend hours planning a youth group session, put in loads of thought and effort, deliver it with energy and enthusiasm, and yet the best part of the session is so often the washing-up at the end, when one or two will come through to the kitchen to help. That's when the real conversations happen. That's when the young people tell their stories and talk about whatever is concerning them, their hopes and their dreams.

I remember chatting with the youth pastor at a church I was attending. At that time she was busy repainting the room where the young people met, and, as it was the summer holiday time, some of them were coming to help. As we talked about the progress being made with the decorating, her main reflection was that some of the best conversations she'd had since taking up the role of youth pastor happened during that week of being knee-deep in dustsheets and paint.

That's the way it is, always has been and, I'm guessing, always will be. It's when we're getting on with the ordinary business of life alongside others that we start to talk deeply about life and faith. That's why mentoring works – because, fundamentally, it's about relationship. It builds on this natural phenomenon, deliberately and intentionally making it part of life, not just a one-off for those who wander into the kitchen or are free to paint a room. It's about taking the time not just to educate young people in the things of God, but to show them what following God is like in ordinary times, helping them to recognise where God is at work in their lives and how he wants to use them for the purposes of his kingdom.

Part II

Mentoring teenagers

4

The changing world of adolescence

Incarnational youth ministry requires us to view adolescence as a mission field. In this case, the mission field is a life stage rather than a spot on the globe, but it is often every bit as foreign to us as unfamiliar geography.[1]

One of my most mortifying moments happened during my second-year teaching practice placement. I can still remember it vividly. It was a Thursday afternoon and I had a class of 34 Year 4 pupils in a small mobile classroom. During that particular week, the school was undergoing an OFSTED inspection, and I had been informed that an inspector would be sitting in on my lessons that afternoon.

The bell rang to mark the end of lunch time and in marched the 34 children... with half a worm. Now, as you can imagine, 34 eight-year-olds and half a worm in a small classroom don't make for a peaceful introduction to the afternoon's lessons. There was shrieking and entrails and all sorts of chaos, and, under the pressure of knowing that the OFSTED inspector would be arriving at any moment, I heard myself saying, 'Class 4B, you're behaving like children!' The room fell silent. Then one child bravely ventured the response, 'But... we are children.'

How do you respond to those words of wisdom? I couldn't believe I had come out with such a ridiculous statement! Here was I, someone who'd spent a number of years talking about the importance of understanding the ages and stages and therefore the behaviour of children, undoing all that talk in one brief sentence.

Young people today

Young people tend to come in for quite a lot of bad press. Back in 2008, Mark Easton, BBC News Home Editor, wrote in his blog:

> Reading the great British press, one might be forgiven for thinking that all our teenagers are binge-drinking, drug-addled, knife-wielding thugs ready to leap out and stab a granny for a fiver. There is a real problem with knife-crime in some parts of the UK, let's not pretend otherwise. And there are many other problems concerning young people in this country. But I thought it might be timely to remind ourselves that youth doesn't necessarily mean yob.[2]

He then went on to list ten reasons why we should celebrate teenagers in the UK, including the fact that teenagers are more likely to do voluntary work than people from any other generation. In fact, they are ten times more likely to be volunteering in our communities than regularly being antisocial in them. This still holds true today.

This is a social group that is actually happier, achieving at a higher level, with better health and more opportunity for travel, sport and cultural activities than any previous generation in our history.

If we are to mentor young people effectively, however, we need to take the time to understand the world in which they are growing up, familiarising ourselves with the characteristics of this life stage, so that we can help them navigate the sometimes uncertain terrain from childhood to adulthood. It is no longer enough to think back to when we were their age: the world has changed beyond recognition and the challenges that they encounter on a daily basis are quite different.

It probably comes as no surprise to hear that young people are living in a rapidly changing world, both internally and externally. They are bombarded with change and choices, and they desperately need adults who are willing to help them make sense of what's going on around them and within them. Young people have many questions and often don't fully understand even themselves – which can lead to a lot of confusion and misunderstanding on all sides.

A changing world

Over the next few pages I want to spend some time looking at this changing world. Obviously, in this short space we can only paint some broad brushstrokes, and cannot really take into account the wide age span involved, but I hope I can give some insight into the world with which young people today are engaging and the way the landscape has changed since previous generations.

Social changes

Freedoms and restrictions

There is a real paradox apparent during the adolescent years in that most young people today experience both more freedom and more restriction, particularly in the earlier teenage years. They live in a world of information technology and navigate it without effort – texting, visiting social networking sites, with live chat and virtual meet-ups as a normal part of their world, often using language that is indecipherable to non-teens.

In their social networking world they are largely independent and often free from any sort of adult presence, restriction or understanding. In the 'real world', however, many teenagers experience far greater restrictions than previous generations because of parental fears about their physical safety. As a result, many teenagers are less free to travel on their own and are ferried from activity to activity.

While this greater restriction applies to many teenagers growing up today, we must acknowledge that the converse is true for some. In some communities, even very young teenagers are left to wander freely and may find themselves caring for younger family members.

This helps to highlight another social change. There have always been those who have plenty and those who have less in terms of material prosperity, but the gap between the two is now glaringly wide, and many teenagers are very much aware that they are excluded from the opportunities enjoyed by their peers. This exclusion can be seen in the material goods they are able to own, sometimes in the education they receive, and quite often in their access to technology.

Aspirations

A quick glance at many of the magazines that line newsagents' shelves will reveal headlines shouting to us about a large number of young people who are making huge sums of money, some of whom have found fame and fortune overnight through appearing on a reality TV show or becoming a top model or sporting star, or through becoming an influencer through their Instagram account or YouTube channel. This has had a huge effect on the aspirations of many young people. They have seen others no different from themselves achieve that status, so why shouldn't they?

Family life

Depending on cultural background, parents have children either earlier than previous generations or later, after establishing careers. Families with two breadwinners have disposable income but may spend less time at home. Social structures have changed, with even more young people today experiencing family breakdown and/or living in blended families. In some parts of the country, they are now less likely to live in the same geographic area as their extended family, resulting in less contact with members of different generations.

Education

Teenagers today think, engage and discover in ways that would have been alien to previous generations, with the Internet opening up a vast world of exploration and relationship. They are taught to take greater responsibility for their own learning and to question and challenge what they are told. To those of us who haven't experienced this approach to education, their questioning can sometimes seem rude or precocious, but it's not meant to be. They simply want to get to the heart of what is being said.

Personal changes

Puberty

During the teenage years, young people make the journey through puberty to maturity in the same way as previous generations. The difference today is that puberty is starting much earlier. Research carried out in 2006 by the John Moores University Centre for Public Health has found that the age of the onset of puberty has been coming down for the past 150 years.

There are a number of reasons given for this change: better nutrition and health care, but also increased stress, are considered to be factors. Early-onset puberty can have negative effects, such as the risk of missing some important aspects of emotional development and leaping forward into a whole new arena of life experience. It can also affect the self-esteem of 'late' developers, who may feel left behind.

Emotional upheaval

It seems that young people today encounter more issues that affect them emotionally than previous generations did, and conversations around mental health are now at the forefront of our life together. As we know, many of the pressures that young people face stem from life now being played out equally 'in real life' and online through the plethora of social media sites.

In her article, *10 Most Common Problems Teens Face in 2021*,[3] author Jennifer Waddle lists the following as key issues that teenagers struggle with or experience:

- Acceptance
- Stress – largely relating to school, parents/carers and peer pressure
- Depression and anxiety

- Self-harm
- Bullying
- Desensitisation
- Sex
- Disrespect
- Trust – particularly of authority figures
- Motivation.

I would also want to add into this list the whole area of gender identity and issues around climate change. Teenagers are being exposed to, and are directly facing, bigger and bigger issues at younger and younger ages – issues that can be hugely confusing, not just for young people, and that require complex thought.

It would also appear that this generation is marked by a sense of abandonment by adults, which leaves young people alone to navigate the difficulties and increases the pressure that they feel.

Spiritual changes

One further area where there has been significant change over recent years is that of spirituality. Young people are open and willing to talk about spiritual matters, and are very much wanting spiritual experience. The problem is that they are looking for this experience pretty much everywhere except in the church:

> In the climate of 'creating a god that works for you' church, traditional religions and the promise of heaven are out of style. Shared experiences, spirituality and the potential of humanity are definitely in. Absolute truth claims, whether moral or religious, are out. Personalised belief systems and pragmatic moral commitments are in. Discovering a transcendent God who seeks to communicate his will is out. Experiencing a domesticated god who wants persons to fulfil themselves is in. In short, Yahweh is no longer an acceptable God for our culture – he is being left behind in search of more favourable alternatives.[4]

The teenagers in our churches are growing up in this climate and are just as susceptible to the 'pick and mix' culture as their non-churched peers. The teenage years are a key time for faith development, when everything is up for question. It's as if, for many of them, the slate has been wiped clean and they're gathering again the things that they believe. They are asking difficult questions about faith, and particularly about why they believe what they do. Is it simply because of the family they were born into?

Missionaries into a new culture

What is our role as mentors in all this? I believe we have a crucial role to play in walking alongside young people as they ask their questions, as they work through their emotions and as they make decisions for their futures.

We need to rethink ourselves as missionaries entering a new culture, making sure we are clear about what the unchanging word of God has to say to a young person growing up in an ever-changing world. As Richard Dunn puts it:

> The pacing-then-leading adult acts as a translator of truth into the vernacular of the adolescent's experience. Leading does not seek to tell them what to think, feel or do. Leading rather translates and communicates truth in a way that is meaningful in the midst of the adolescent's thoughts, feelings and choices.[5]

Our role is not to rescue young people from their culture but to help to equip them for life within it. That is where God is, but sometimes young people (and adults) need assistance in seeing where he is at work. Neither is our role to adopt the culture of young people. Kenda Creasy Dean, a practitioner and theologian in youth ministry, puts it helpfully: 'One sign of healthy adult leadership is the ability to be one with youth without becoming one of them. They know how and when to say unapologetically, "You are fourteen, I'm not".'

Young people need to be assured that faith is not about a single experience of God but a succession of occasions in which God meets with us, we respond to him and, by his Holy Spirit, he changes us. And young people need adults who will walk this road with them in real relationship, not because such relationships are good for them at their stage of development but simply because relationships demonstrate something of who God is.

We will never be able to talk people into spiritual maturity. We need to demonstrate what maturity looks like, engage in meaningful discussion, share our struggles and provide young people with the tools for making good decisions, pray for them, point out to them how God is at work in their lives and be there to pick up the pieces when life doesn't go quite right.

As we have already seen, what's amazing about this is that, in the process, we will also find ourselves learning with them and from them.

5

Creating a safe environment

We are to love those we mentor and show them that they must have as their first and foremost relationship, a connection with their heavenly Father, not with us.[1]

When talking about mentoring teenagers, I am frequently asked how it fits within a safeguarding policy. Is it possible to meet one-to-one with a young person and still be following safeguarding guidelines?

The answer is most definitely yes, but it does require some careful thought. Procedures and accountability structures are a healthy and necessary part of mentoring in today's church. They are there to protect both adults and young people, not to prevent healthy and appropriate relationships between the generations. Rather than being seen as rules that constrain us, they should be seen as guidelines that free us to be safe and beyond reproach.

Safeguarding and DBS

All churches should have their own safeguarding policy, which should ideally include guidelines for one-to-one work with children and young people. Your church's named Safeguarding Officer should be clear about the guidelines for these situations. If your church's policy doesn't cover safeguarding clearly and adequately, your policy will need updating. This can be done by contacting the relevant diocesan or denominational staff who will inform you on what the child safeguarding guidelines are.

Everyone who wishes to work with young people must be clear about the safeguarding policy and able to adhere to it, and have a current DBS (Disclosure and Barring Service) clearance certificate. All safeguarding policies also need to give very clear details of procedures that must be followed regarding confidentiality.

Confidentiality

Very occasionally, an issue will arise in the mentoring situation that we feel should be passed on to someone else. Young people need to know that we are not going to discuss with their parents, carers or youth leaders everything that we discuss with them, but at the same time we must be careful not to promise complete confidentiality. If we believe, from what our mentoree has told us, that they are in danger of harm, either from themselves or from someone else, or that they have been harmed in some way, that information needs to be passed on initially to the Safeguarding Officer within the church.

It's important, right from the start of a mentoring relationship, to be clear with your mentoree about what confidentiality means in a situation like this. I tend to start by making a statement such as, 'You need to know that anything you tell me will stay between us. I won't be giving your youth leader or parents or carers an update on what we've talked about. However, if I'm concerned that you or another person may be at risk of harm, I will need to talk to someone else.' I then make sure that the mentoree understands what I've said and we proceed from there.

Obviously the age of the young person involved does affect matters slightly. Mentoring a 13-year-old is quite different from mentoring a 19-year-old, who would be considered to be an adult. This does not put us outside the good practice guidelines, however.

If a conversation has taken place that has raised some concern for you, it is important to make written notes immediately after the conversation has finished, recording the date, time and location, what was said and also anything that was communicated non-verbally. In fact, keeping notes on all your mentoring conversations is a good plan anyway, enabling you to keep track of what you have talked about and any goals you may have set.

As well as the official safeguarding information, there are some other guidelines that we can follow to help ensure good practice.

Gender issues

There are mixed opinions on whether boys should be mentored only by men, and girls by women, and of course this is becoming an increasingly complex conversation. Some would say that it's not really an issue and, in fact, most local authorities don't see it as a major concern. My feeling is that, on the whole, it is best to have same-sex mentoring relationships, for a number of reasons, but mainly because mentoring is partly about being a role model to the young person, and that can best be provided by someone of the same sex. Particularly in the area of leadership, young women have fewer role models, so less idea of what it is like to be a woman in leadership. Awareness of role models is a vital part of growing in leadership.

However, where you are aware that gender identity is, or may be, an issue for the young person involved, please ensure that you take guidance and advice from both the young person's parents or carers, and your Safeguarding Officer, and wherever possible, the young person themselves, asking what is most helpful and supportive to them.

Overseen but not overheard

One of the main difficulties about mentoring teenagers is the question of where to meet. You want to be in a place where you can have a good conversation without fear of being overheard, but safeguarding guidelines make it very clear that you and your mentoree should never be alone together in a non-public place. A good general rule is that we look for places where we can be overseen but not overheard.

What works best, then, is to meet in a place where you are able to have a private conversation but where you can be seen by others. Coffee shops, cafés, the family home (but only when the family are around) and public parks are all good places. Some churches make a room available at specific times when a number of mentors and mentorees can meet at the same time. Wherever you meet, always make sure that your mentoree's parents or carers know where the young person is and that he or she is with you.

When training youth leaders, I suggest to them that they imagine having to make a phone call to a parent explaining what's happening at any given moment, or, taking it a step further, to try out the explanation and add 'Your Honour' at the end! If you wouldn't feel totally comfortable about explaining to a parent or a judge what's going on, it's a good indication that it needs changing.

Parents and carers

It goes without saying that parents and carers are key when embarking on a mentoring relationship. Mentoring young people within the context of a Mentoring Programme provides a healthy and supervised infrastructure for good relationships to be established, and transparent communication to happen. Some parents or carers may be a little suspicious at first about what's happening, or may be anxious that their child is about to spill all the family secrets. Within the programme, mentors should be made aware that they need to make sure that they keep open communication with the mentoree's parents or carers about when and where they are meeting and the nature of what's being discussed, without disclosing the actual content. It's often useful to make it clear to the carers that they are free to contact you at any time.

Personal boundaries

Boundaries are a fine line to walk. On the one hand, I have been arguing that mentoring teenagers should be about sharing your life. There is a place for boundaries, however. Young people need to know that you are there for them, that you care for them, and that you want them to know you as a person, too, but they shouldn't become overdependent on you. We need to set realistic boundaries so that they don't expect attention or time from us that we cannot and should not give.

This works the other way around as well. As mentors, we need to respect the boundaries of the young people we are mentoring. This means ensuring that our behaviour is consistently appropriate. They might not want us interrupting them when they're with friends, or constantly getting in touch with them between meetings. It also means not trying to meet their every need ourselves.

Use of technology

Technology and social media can be a marvellous tool, allowing us to be in touch so much quicker and more immediately than in days gone by. Texting is an excellent way of following up prayer requests or a reminder about when you're meeting, or to ask how things are going. These are some good-practice guidelines that mentors should follow:

- Keep a log stating with whom and when they communicated.
- Keep a log of significant text or online conversations.
- Save text messages as text files where possible and make young people aware that they are doing this.
- Use technology at appropriate hours of the day, agreeing lengths of time and curfews with young people (for example, not after 10.00 pm or before 9.00 am).
- Pass on or show any texts or online conversations that raise concerns to their line manager or supervisor.
- Use clear language, avoiding words or abbreviations which might be misinterpreted.

And guidelines for the use of social media:

- Avoid 'lone working' in the online world. Practically, this means avoiding direct messaging between adults and young people.
- Maintain appropriate boundaries in the online world. Just as in the offline world, it is important to keep a distinction between our private lives and our work within church, and to pay particular attention to the dynamics of power and influence.
- Do not use personal social media accounts to contact young people. The simplest way to observe the above two precautions is to avoid having leaders and young people as 'friends' on social media. It is far preferable to have an official account for the group in question, and to ask young people to 'like' that page. Any news about group events or anything else can be posted on that page. More than one leader should have access to this page, providing for accountability and transparency. Conversations between leaders and young people should happen in the public section of these pages (such as the 'wall' or in comments under posts) where everyone can see them, rather than via direct messages.
- Behave in the online world as you would offline. Simply put, if you would not say it offline, do not say it online! This includes posting links to offensive or otherwise inappropriate content, making comments about someone's appearance that could be interpreted as either sexual or offensive, or 'liking' inappropriate content on social media.
- Treat online 'consent' the same as offline 'consent'. You will need the consent of the individual and/or their parents or carers to use and store photographs, to retain any information relating to them online, and so on. It is a good idea to make their parents or carers aware of the social media that your church uses and ensure that you have their consent to their child's usage.[2]

Again, in all of this, please be informed by, and adhere to, your church's Safeguarding Policy in relation to the use of messaging and social media.

Accountability

All being well, you will be working as a mentor as part of the youth ministry in your church, so you will naturally be under the supervision of the youth leader. However, if this isn't the situation, for whatever reason (your church doesn't have a youth leader; your church only has a couple of young people and you want to encourage them; you're working with a young person outside your church situation), please do find someone to whom you can be accountable and still be as transparent about what is happening as you would under a formal programme. This could be a church leader or an appropriate godly friend. It's good to keep them informed about when you're meeting and how you feel the sessions are going.

Stop, look and listen

Young people need safe people to be their mentors, people who are following God first, before they seek to lead others. All of us, even the best of us, need to follow common-sense guidelines to keep us completely beyond reproach.

Bo Boshers and Judson Poling suggest the following framework as a helpful way of checking the situations that we are in:

- Stop: to ask if this is a wise activity.
- Look: to make sure someone else is around.
- Listen: to your gut and to the Holy Spirit for warnings about what you're doing.[3]

Please do not be put off by all these guidelines and warnings. As mentioned earlier, they are there to protect, not prevent. Mentoring young people is a richly rewarding experience for all involved and, with just a little bit of thought and attention, it can happen easily and well.

6

Putting a mentoring scheme in place

If Christ lives in us, controlling our personalities, we will leave glorious marks on the lives we touch. Not because of our lovely characters, but because of his.[1]

I hope, by now, you are convinced that mentoring is a good plan, one of the most effective ways of building leaders for both today and tomorrow and of growing mature young disciples. If there are just a couple of young people in your church, mentoring can happen quite spontaneously and organically (while following the guidelines in chapter 5!). If there is a greater number of potential mentorees, however, a more organised approach will be useful.

In this chapter I shall outline the process used to establish the church-based mentoring scheme that I mentioned earlier. Of course, this isn't the only way of doing it; it's simply the way that seemed to work for us, so I offer it here in the hope that it may help you get the ball rolling.

For the purpose of this chapter I'm going to assume that you are the person who will be instrumental in setting up the scheme. Your role is key as the person who holds the vision and communicates it to others. You will have something of a prophetic role, as well as being an advocate for young people and reminding the church of its mandate to raise the next generation in discipleship and for leadership.

If you are to convince others of the benefits of mentoring, however, you need to be giving time to it yourself, by both mentoring a young person and, if possible, being mentored yourself. You need to be convinced that mentoring is worthy of time and energy, and be willing to demonstrate that conviction in your own life.

Define your mentoring scheme

It's important to be clear in your own mind about who the mentoring scheme is for and what you hope to achieve through it.

When we first set up our mentoring scheme, the target group was the whole youth group. I wanted all of the young people to have the opportunity to meet one-to-one with an older disciple. As time went on, however, it became clear that a number of them had very clear leadership gifts and we wanted to help them develop those gifts. As a result, we became far more intentional about linking those young people up with adults who would not only mentor them but who had leadership gifts themselves and could give real opportunities for the young people to begin to use their gifts.

Sometimes people shy away from offering a mentoring scheme only to those with potential leadership ability, and I can understand that. The last thing we want is to discriminate against people who don't have leadership gifts but still need to grow as disciples. There may well be room for you, as there was for us, to run schemes for potential leaders and others. But I think it's far better to be clear in your aim and run a small scheme well, rather than have a free-for-all that ends up being ineffective because of its lack of clarity.

Some church traditions have started to use mentoring as a rite of passage. In fact, for many years now it has been incorporated into the youth ministries of numerous Mennonite churches. Following the model of Jesus, at the age of twelve, leaving his parents to focus on the temple (Luke 2:41–50), the Mennonites link an adult member of the church with a young person on their twelfth birthday, identifying this as a significant step towards maturity. In our culture we have very few, if any, rites of passage, for young people to mark their journey from childhood into adulthood. Mentoring can provide a good opportunity to mark a significant time of life.

I'm also hearing of more and more churches, particularly across Europe, that are using mentoring as part of their confirmation courses. These courses may last for a whole year, including mission trips and opportunities to share the stories of what God is doing in individual lives, as well as the normal confirmation material. The result is that young people are discipled well, they are given genuine opportunities to serve and they have an adult on hand to encourage them, share their questions and act constantly as a pointer to God.

An important question to ask at this point, then, is 'How will the scheme fit within the existing youth ministry, and the ministry of the youth?' It's essential to think this through if the scheme is to be fully integrated into the life of the church. Some questions to consider are:

- Will the mentoring scheme replace the existing youth ministry, or will it be an addition to it?
- Do I have the support of the overall church leadership?
- Will the scheme conflict with anything else that is happening?
- Are we going to have to stop something else in order for mentoring to happen?
- Who is going to take responsibility for heading up the scheme? The youth team? Another adult not involved in youth ministry? A parent? A young person?

It is also good to think through your own role as the person setting up the scheme. Consider such issues as:

- How much time do I need to commit?
- Will I provide the material for discussion?
- Am I just a friend to listen to them?
- Do I provide practical opportunities for the mentoree to work alongside me in leadership?

Taking time to address these issues at the start will save much frustration further down the line.

Set realistic goals

When we first offered mentoring to the youth group, I have to confess that more than a few were quite hesitant about it. What made the difference was that a couple of the group were already being mentored and loving it, and the rest of the group could see opportunities for leadership opening up for those few, so they were willing to give it a try too. It may be worth starting with just a handful of young people, identifying those who you think will benefit from some training in leadership and who will be good advocates to others.

Depending on the size of your church and the number of young people you have, set realistic goals for the number you want to be involved with in the first year.

Casting the vision

Once you are clear about who the scheme is for and what its focus is, it's time to start 'casting the vision' to the church – sharing what you plan to do – and recruiting potential mentors. Do this in every possible way you can imagine: upfront presentation, interviewing young people who are already involved, sharing stories from other churches that have adopted this model of youth ministry, and identifying people who you think would make good mentors and inviting them to take part.

A lesson that I have to learn on a regular basis is that just because I'm excited about something, it doesn't necessarily mean that others are going to jump on board immediately. A vision needs to be shared on a number of occasions before people even hear it properly, so be ready to do more than a one-off presentation.

In our church, we combined several approaches. First we ran a sermon series on 'Children, young people and the kingdom' because we felt it was important to address the question of the place that children and young people have in the kingdom of God. Are they disciples in waiting or disciples in training? Following on from that, I did a presentation about our hopes for the mentoring scheme and invited the congregation to take away a leaflet to reflect on and pray about. I also wrote to people that I very much wanted to see involved, and asked the young people themselves if there was anyone they would like me to contact on their behalf.

We found that the personal invitation was by far the most effective way of recruiting. Often, when a blanket invitation is given, many people won't hear it for themselves, especially if they don't see themselves as someone who's 'good with young people'. Giving a blanket invitation is important, however, because there may be people you overlook because you simply don't know them. I am so thankful that a number of people responded to our blanket request who turned out to be brilliant mentors but had never crossed my path personally as potential recruits.

I should add a word of caution, though. Just because someone responds to the invitation, it doesn't necessarily mean that they are right for the role, and in my experience there will always be one or two who you won't be sure about. We made it clear that a response to the invitation did not guarantee being linked up with a young person. In order to make these decisions well, it's worth having more than one person involved in discerning who may or may not be appropriate.

Training your mentors

Once we had recruited our first batch of mentors, we brought them together for a training session, looking at a lot of the material that has gone into this book. We explored what mentoring was, how we can help young people explore their gifts and provide them with meaningful opportunities to lead, the characteristics of a mentor and how to ask good questions. We set out our expectations of them and the support that they could expect from us. We also talked through the 'safe from harm' guidelines.

Once the training is complete, you may want to introduce the mentors to the rest of the church and have an opportunity in a service to commission them and pray for them.

Inviting the young people to take part

A mentoring scheme doesn't get too far without any mentorees, so it's time to start sharing the vision with the young people whom you would like to be involved. This might be as an open offer to the whole youth group, or you may want to identify those with specific leadership gifts, depending on the focus of your scheme. Don't worry about how others will respond if they don't get invited. We found that the invitation stage was an excellent opportunity to have good conversations with young people about what we were doing and about what they wanted to do. It brought forward a number of them who were serious about being discipled on issues other than leadership, which meant that we could sort that out for them.

Linking young people and mentors

Matching up mentors with mentorees requires quite a bit of discernment. Take some time to pray, preferably with others, about who to link with whom. Once we had done this, we invited everybody to meet together so that we could make the introductions and they could have their first 'getting to know you' session.

We asked each pair to commit to meet together for three months and to review at the end of that period whether or not the relationship was working. For the most part, things worked out well – mostly, I think, because of the time we took to ask God to show us which relationships would link up smoothly. There were a couple that didn't really connect, however, so after three months we rematched them. I'm so glad that we had the three-month review as it meant that people didn't feel as if they had failed if the relationship didn't work out; we'd flagged up at the start that sometimes some personalities simply don't connect well.

Providing ongoing support

It's good to have regular opportunities to be in touch with mentors and mentorees to see how it's going and to provide resources to help the mentors grow in their mentoring skills. We recommended books on mentoring, or gave them some helpful questions to ask or issues for reflection. A combination of meeting with all the mentors together and giving time for personal one-to-one conversations is an effective way of encouraging and supporting your mentors and providing healthy oversight.

Dealing with problems

When mentoring goes well, it is one of the most encouraging relationships to be part of but, as we have seen, occasionally it doesn't go quite to plan. Difficulties tend to arise for a number of key reasons.

- Lack of agreement: Both mentor and mentoree should be clear from the outset about what they have committed themselves to and what the expectations are. 'Meeting up to discuss things' is too vague and does not imply a proper mentoring relationship.
- Lack of contact: Mentoring takes time, and a mentoring relationship will soon die if a mentor can't spare the time to meet up. The same applies if the young person feels that they have too many commitments, with school and other activities. Again, being clear from the start about what is expected prevents this frustration. If a mentor really doesn't have time to commit on a regular basis, or knows that they're going to end up cancelling meetings quite frequently, they should wait until they do have the time (and maybe think about whether

there's something they could give up for a while in order to be committed to mentoring).

- Lack of openness: Unless both parties are prepared to talk honestly and openly, not much growth is going to happen. Mentors should be willing to share appropriately about themselves, as the more open they are, the more likely it is that their mentorees will follow suit. Please note the word 'appropriately', however! Discussing their marriage problems or their dislike of the vicar may not be the most helpful approach! (Actually, if either of those things are a problem, it may be good for the mentor to find someone to talk to.)
- Lack of direction: Both parties need to be clear about the goals of the mentoring relationship, and how they are going to reach those goals. It's good to review every few months what progress has been made.

All these pitfalls can be avoided if a clear framework is provided from the outset for both the mentor and the mentoree, and both are committed to giving time to make the relationship work.

In part III, we are going to spend some time thinking about how we can play our role to the best of our ability and in a God-honouring and effective way. The appendix to this book (pages 115–120) gives a practical outline of how you might conduct the first meeting to establish a mentoring scheme and then some suggestions for further meetings.

Part III

On being a mentor

7

The characteristics of a mentor

We teach what we know but we reproduce who we are.[1]

A while ago I was leading a seminar for a group of churches. Among the group was someone I've known for quite a long time, and at the end of the session he greeted me with the words, 'I can so see who's mentored you!' He had no definite knowledge of who that person was, but he thought he could recognise in the way I did things, the way I spoke, and probably even in the hand gestures I used, something of the person who has influenced me and taught me so much about what I now do – and he was spot on!

I also remember very clearly the time when members of the youth group that I led started to lead services themselves. Watching them was like looking in a mirror. In full technicolour I could see all my mannerisms and hear all my turns of phrase. I have to admit that it made me very aware of things about me that needed to change!

In chapter 1 we looked at how Paul exhorted the Christians in Corinth to follow his example as he followed the example of Christ (1 Corinthians 11:1). If you're anything like me, your first response is, 'As if I could ever ask anyone to do that!' Let's not forget, though, that this is the same Paul who declares himself 'the worst sinner of all' (1 Timothy 1:15), and who, in his letter to the church in Rome, bemoans the fact that the good he wants to do, he doesn't do, and the bad he doesn't want to do, he just keeps on doing (Romans 7:15).

Despite this, he is still able to encourage others to imitate him as he imitates Christ. Let's be encouraged by that! Paul knows that the priority is who it is that he is following, who it is that he is imitating. That's what gives him the courage to be able to say, 'Imitate me'. When we ourselves have that courage in place, we'll be able to say to those whom we lead and mentor, 'If you want to know what it looks like to be a disciple of Jesus, if you want to know what it means to be a leader in God's kingdom, then take a look at my life, because of who I'm following.'

It would be easy to stop there and just encourage young people to look at our lives, but of course that's not the whole picture, and it wasn't for Paul, either. Throughout his travels and his teaching, Paul consistently pointed people to Jesus. We too need to hold these two things in tension, knowing that the young people will be looking at our lives very closely, and there needs to be good practice there for them to copy. Mentoring is not about making them clones of us, however. Our task is to keep on demonstrating that we are who we are because of who Jesus is, and to help the young people find their identity in him.

In his first letter to Timothy, Paul sets out a number of character qualities that Timothy needs to develop in himself and to identify in others who are stepping into leadership. This letter is a good place for us to start as we look at the characteristics of a godly mentor. It is about the qualities of a leader rather than of a mentor, but, if we are mentoring young people in leadership, they need to see in us the qualities of a leader.

The characteristics that Paul highlights fit into three main categories: qualities of the person in relationship to God, in relationship to themselves, and in relationship to other people. You might want to stop for a moment, get hold of a Bible and read the whole of 1 Timothy to see the sweep of Paul's argument.

Here are some of the qualities that he mentions.

In relationship to God

Christ-centred

> Cling tightly to your faith in Christ.
> 1 TIMOTHY 1:19

This is the foundational quality for a Christian mentor. First and foremost, mentors themselves need to be disciples, rooted in Christ and daily deepening their own relationship with him. We need to be people whose trust is firmly placed in the saving work of Christ so that we can build others in their commitment to Christ and not to ourselves.

In John 15:5, Jesus tells us that without him we can do nothing. That's a strong statement, and maybe in the back of your mind you're wondering if it is really true: 'Can I really do nothing?' I can think of plenty of things that I can do, but the point Jesus is making is that if you want to do anything of lasting value, anything that is fruitful for God's kingdom, it can only happen as we keep him at the centre of all we do.

Spiritually fit

> Do not waste time arguing over godless ideas and old wives' tales. Spend your time and energy in training yourself for spiritual fitness. Physical exercise has some value, but spiritual exercise is much more important, for it promises a reward in both this life and the next.
> 1 TIMOTHY 4:7–8

This links into the previous characteristic, because if we want to stay Christ-centred we need to train ourselves to do so. Christ-centredness and godliness don't grow in us by accident. We need to be purposeful about pursuing those qualities, and that's where spiritual disciplines come in. Through many generations, this is how godly people have exercised spiritually. Much has been written on spiritual disciplines, and I would recommend taking some time to read one of the current books on the subject (please look at the bibliography for some suggestions). In short, there are two kinds of spiritual disciplines: disciplines of abstinence and disciplines of engagement. Richard Foster lists them as the following:

Abstinence	Engagement
Solitude	Study
Silence	Worship
Fasting	Celebration
Frugality	Service
Chastity	Prayer
Secrecy	Fellowship
Sacrifice	Confession

Foster suggests that rather than attempting to practise all these disciplines at once, it's worth focusing on one or two for a few months, and, as that pattern of discipline becomes established, concentrate on another one or two.[2]

An identity rooted in God

> But you, Timothy, belong to God, so run from all these evil things.
> 1 TIMOTHY 6:11

Paul gives this instruction to Timothy just after he's warned him about people who follow false teachers and those who are concerned solely with money and wealth. It's as if he is saying to Timothy, 'To avoid getting caught up in these things, you need to remember who and whose you are. You belong to God so your life should be different.' If we forget that as our starting point, it's not long before we find ourselves in trouble.

If we're serious about growing as a mentor, we need to take the time to remember who and whose we are. If we fail to do that, we'll find that we start doing everything in order to earn other people's approval, which is just exhausting and will get in the way of listening to God. Above and beyond anything else, we are God's people, his children, and that needs to be our primary focus. God's intention is that as we lead other people, we make it our priority to follow him closely. It's amazing how quickly we can find our identity in the roles that we play rather than in God.

One of my most sobering moments in relation to this issue came as I was driving a minibus full of young people home from a weekend away in the Lake District. We'd had a fantastic time together, and it was so good to hear the chatter and singing and laughter coming from the group. We'd been travelling for a little while when one of the group leant forward to talk to me. She told me that she'd just been praying for me and felt that God wanted me to know that he loved the role I played as youth pastor, and the concern that I had for the group, but he'd really like to meet Ruth again.

As I reflected, I realised that she was right. Whenever I opened my Bible, it was to prepare a message for the group; whenever I prayed, it was to pray for the members of the group. My whole identity had become that of 'youth pastor' and God had to remind me that first and foremost I was Ruth, disciple of Jesus. It's not that what I was doing was wrong; it's just that I'd got my starting point confused.

Bible-centred

> Focus on reading the Scriptures to the church, encouraging the believers, and teaching them.
>
> 1 TIMOTHY 4:13

One of the most important gifts that we have to offer our mentorees is our love for the Bible. It is vital for young people to know that our lifestyle and the choices we make are guided by the Bible. The Christian teaching that we share is not just a collection of nice thoughts, but is inspired by what we learn from the Bible, revealed to us by the Holy Spirit. The only way in which we can pass on our love for the Bible is if we genuinely love it, listen to it and live it. Youthwork magazine contributor John Allan makes the point:

> One end result of all mentoring should be a deeper respect for God's Word and more confidence in consulting it. Whatever you teach, teach it from the Bible. Build dependence, not upon your wisdom, but upon the Word of God.[3]

In relationship to themselves

Self-controlled

> They must exercise self-control.
> 1 TIMOTHY 3:11

On a number of occasions, Paul talks about the need to be self-controlled. Dr Ted Engstrom and Dr Ron Jenson suggest that 'keeping your life and mentoring in balance involves disciplining your use of time and resources, and keeping free from distractions and sin'.[4]

Discipline in the use of time is an area where I have to work hard. I put it down to being creative and spontaneous, but that's just an excuse for allowing myself to be distracted. I tend to have a plan about whatever I want or need to get done, but if something else comes along that looks more fun, you can guarantee that I'll be leading the way in joining in.

A number of years ago I had a line manager who taught me so much about being disciplined with time. Each day he had a very clear list of what needed to be accomplished, and was great at getting it all done. If a meeting was due to start at 9.00 am, it would start at 9.00 am. If I sent him an email, he would respond within a set timeframe. You always knew where you were with him: if he had promised something, he would deliver it, and that helped colleagues to feel valued by him.

We are fallen people living in a fallen world, and I have yet to meet someone who is managing to live a totally sinless life. At the same time, we need to be aware of those areas in our lives that can easily trip us up. Sadly, sin has the ability to render us ineffective in our mentoring, so, both for our own sake and for the sake of those we mentor, we need to keep short accounts with God about our lives, so that we can live in a way that honours him.

Integrity

> [They] must be well respected and have integrity.
> 1 TIMOTHY 3:8

Integrity is about being people whose words match the actions in our lives, and it is one of the greatest needs in leadership. Young people very quickly see through us when what we are saying to them is not matched by our lives in practice. Integrity is about being the same person no matter what the situation, whether we're at work, socialising with non-Christian friends or at church. Young people need to see their mentors living lives of integrity so they can work out what integrity would look like in their own lives. Being a Christian at school or college is probably one of the hardest challenges, and, if we are to encourage them not to live a double life but to be true to their faith, we need to be demonstrating it ourselves.

In relationship to others

Giving an example to other believers

> Don't let anyone think less of you because you are young. Be an example to all believers in what you say, in the way you live, in your love, your faith, and your purity.
> 1 TIMOTHY 4:12

Paul was aware that Timothy was a young leader and that older people might look down on him because of his age. He encourages Timothy not to let others think less of him because of this, but to be confident that his life can be an example to them. I think Paul would say the same to us, too, no matter what our age. We can be examples to other believers by the way that we live, through our faith and by the way we serve others. When Paul says, 'Be an example', the Greek words he uses literally mean to 'print yourself' on others, to leave an impression on them. As John E. Schrock puts it, 'Each day of our lives, we make deposits in the memory banks of those we meet. That becomes our reputation.'

This impression is something that we must pass on to those we mentor. During my time as youth pastor, it was amazing to see how parents and carers in the church were being influenced by their children. They could see their teenagers growing in faith and in commitment to God, so they and other adults in the church were challenged about their own relationships with God.

Hospitable

> [They] must enjoy having guests in [their] home, and... must be able to teach.
> 1 TIMOTHY 3:2b

Mentors are to be relational people – able to establish and maintain healthy relationships with others. They should be able to get alongside young people to encourage them, inspire them and motivate them. As a youth pastor, when looking for new leaders to join the youth team, I would go up to the balcony after the church service and observe which adults the young people were chatting with. I would then approach those adults to ask whether they'd like to explore being part of the team.

Some good questions to ask yourself, then, if you are thinking about mentoring young people, are 'Are they naturally drawn to me and do they want to spend time with me? Do I enjoy being around young people, and are they influenced by me in a good way?'

Gentle

> [They] must be gentle and peace-loving.
> 1 TIMOTHY 3:3b

Mentoring requires a lot of patience and a commitment to the long term. Growth does not happen overnight and young people need someone who will be gentle and patient with them, helping them achieve their best not through criticism but through love, gentleness and affirmation.

This is quite a challenging list of characteristics, and I don't imagine there is anyone who can read through and think they've got it all sorted out. What is required of us, however, is that we are committed to growing more like Christ, and to seeing more of these characteristics in our lives. As Paul wrote, 'I don't mean to say that I have already achieved these things or that I have already reached perfection. But I keep working toward that day when I will finally be all that Christ Jesus saved me for and wants me to be' (Philippians 3:12).

8

Key skills and tools
for mentoring

That's the mentoring model: one person with skills, experience, wisdom, integrity and maturity investing in the life of an eager young learner. There is no better way to invest in the future than by investing ourselves in the life of a young leader-in-training.[1]

Leadership expert John Maxwell has carried out considerable research on the subject of influence. His premise is that, at its most fundamental, leadership is about influence, and that even the most introverted person will influence about 10,000 people in their lifetime. That's quite a phenomenal thought! If that's the level of influence we have without even trying, imagine the impact we could have if we were intentional.

In the previous chapter we looked at the biblical characteristics that a mentor needs to be developing, in order to influence well. We're now going to consider the skills and tools that are useful for being more effective in mentoring.

Praying

Prayer is an essential part of good mentoring and should undergird the whole relationship. I find it quite humbling to know that each day my mentor prays for me. Before we meet, I know that they pray, asking God for wisdom and insight for our time together, and before I leave, they pray with me, bringing to God the issues that we've discussed.

Over the years I have learned so much from them about prayer, and the knowledge of the difference it's made in my life makes me eager to do the same for someone else.

Asking good questions

Asking the right questions, and asking them well, is an important skill for mentors. The mentor's role is to listen to the young people being mentored without passing judgment on them or trying to take responsibility for them – and without trying to mould them into the mentor's likeness. This experience helps mentorees to relax and grow in confidence and trust. It helps them to be honest about their deeper feelings and thoughts. It enables them to perceive their world in new ways and to make progress in their spiritual life.

It's helpful to think through different types of questions and to consider how we can use them.

Open questions are very useful because they encourage the mentoree to engage on a deeper level than is necessary to give a one-word answer. For example, 'What did you enjoy about it?' offers far more scope for response than 'Did you enjoy it?'

Closed questions are best used in short supply, although they are obviously very useful when you just need information. For example, if you want to know whether you are going to meet next Tuesday, all you need is that one-word answer. Using too many closed questions tends to stifle conversation and can end up creating a bit of a Spanish Inquisition atmosphere, but they do have their place.

Reflective questions are probably the crucial questioning tool for mentoring, enabling the mentoree to reflect on previous experiences and get to the heart of how they think and feel.

At the end of this chapter I have included some useful questions that you might want to look through when thinking about your mentoring sessions. I also carry a notebook around with me and have started collecting good questions whenever I hear them.

Active listening

One of the common barriers to proper listening is being distracted by thinking about how we're going to respond to what is being said. When mentoring teenagers, we must be committed to hearing what is being said behind the spoken words, which requires us to focus fully on the young person. We need to be aware of body language, and also to be sensitive to what is not being said. Learning these skills requires patience, humility, sensitivity, acceptance and alertness, but they are such a gift to young people.

Using the Bible

As mentioned in chapter 7, the Bible should be our guiding authority, and the ability to demonstrate how to use the Bible in decision-making and in defining personal values is another important skill for the mentor. Have a Bible available each time you meet and, when appropriate, refer to different verses or passages that could offer some insight into the subject you're discussing.

Affirming

An effective mentor offers the gift of affirmation not only for what is good now but also for the potential they see for the future. Many people would testify that it was the affirmation they received the first time they tried something new that encouraged them to try it again. Affirmation is the soil in which healthy leadership is grown, and also allows for constructive criticism to be offered.

Offering perspective

From their 'outside' vantage point, mentors help young people to see their situation in perspective. Factors influencing the mentor's viewpoint include distance, time, maturity, biblical knowledge, wisdom, experience and differences in personality and gifts.

Challenging

Without honest feedback, direct challenge and loving rebuke, few young leaders will grow into the person God is calling them to be, nor will they fulfil their ministry in the most effective way. There is a fine line to walk, however, between challenging young people far enough and not pushing them beyond where they are ready or able to go.

Although many of us might shy away from challenging a young person, Dr Tim Elmore gives some sound reasons for doing so:

- You want to see them transformed by the power of God.
- The goal is not condemnation but restoration.
- Challenging them to grow must go beyond good advice.
- People need help with the practical application of scriptural truth.
- We must love truth more than anything else in the world.[2]

Enabling good decision-making

The temptation can be quite strong to make decisions for the young person you're mentoring, and, quite often, they will happily let you make them – but that doesn't lead to maturity. We need to let young people make their own decisions, and, if they make mistakes, help them to learn from the experience.

A word of warning

After reading the above, yet again most of us will feel inadequate for the task. That's normal! Each of us will be better at some skills on the list than others. Mentors are not expected to be omnicompetent, but simply to be open to the Spirit and willing to engage in each of these areas in ways that will serve their mentorees.

9

Sharing the journey

Let's not pretend we are there to lead and they are there to follow; rather, we and they are embarking on an adventure together as travelling companions.[1]

What is it about stories that grabs people's attention, no matter what age they are? I find it fascinating to watch people's reactions when I'm teaching, training or preaching. I can be happily talking away and people are listening, but when I start telling a story, either from my own life or someone else's, suddenly everyone is on the edge of their seats, attention caught, wanting to hear more.

I once led a day in a secondary school, the last session in a long day of visiting speakers for the pupils. By that point, it was becoming really hard to keep their focus. My colleague and I started with our material, but everyone was a bit restless so we changed tactic slightly and used a lot more story to illustrate what we were teaching. Suddenly, restlessness was gone and the pupils were focused on what we were saying, wanting to join in with their own stories, too.

There are very few people who don't love a good story. One of the greatest gifts that God has given us to use, not just in mentoring but in so many other situations, is the story of our own lives. As we read through the Bible, we find that it's full of stories of real people, facing real situations and interacting with a real God. I believe that God invites us to add our stories to theirs, demonstrating that he worked in amazing ways in the lives of the people then, and still works in amazing ways in the lives of ordinary people today. We meet and understand each other and God through our own stories.

A shared story

Story is the way God chose to reveal spiritual mysteries to us. Story is the way we learn about each other and our own spiritual journeys. And it is through story that faith communities explain themselves to others. Caring for the souls of our children means sharing God's story with them in creative and appropriate ways. It means sharing our own stories of faith with them in age-appropriate ways. It means helping them understand their own stories. And caring for the souls of our children means incorporating them into the story, the shared experiences and memories, of the community of faith.[2]

Although the paragraph above was written about children, I think it is equally true of teenagers. I also think that it shows how mentoring can come into its own. When mentoring a teenager for leadership, it's easy to get so focused on the task that we forget that ultimately it's all about relationship. It's not just about providing the young person with an opportunity to learn facts and skills; it also offers a chance for them to learn to recognise the story of God in their own lives, and hear something of your story of life with God.

Sharing the story appropriately

Sharing our story with anyone, of any age, requires wisdom and discernment. We must be careful not just to offer the edited highlights, the times when we were at our best, painting ourselves always in a positive light. Young people need to know about the difficult times just as much as about the good, but we should think carefully about how much we share. There are some things that will be too weighty for a young person to carry. For example, it may be quite appropriate to share that you get angry in your marriage at times, but to say that you suspect your spouse of having an affair and that you're thinking of leaving him or her is probably taking it a bit far!

The young people we mentor will be our friends but, as I've already said, they're not our buddies and they're not our peers. The relationship is primarily about focusing on them, and the stories we share should be used for the purpose of helping the young person to discover who they are and how God is at work with them, not taking every opportunity to talk about ourselves and telling the epic of our own lives. Share freely but share wisely!

Sharing in the story of faith

A number of years ago, Peter Brierley carried out a significant piece of research to try to find out why young people were leaving the church in droves. He interviewed many young people between the ages of 8 and 13 (the central age band of those leaving church) to find the answer. Their overwhelming response was that they'd outgrown church, and they felt that God was no longer relevant to them.

That's a tragic indictment of the church – that by the age of twelve, young people feel that they know all there is to know about God and that he no longer has anything to say of relevance to their lives.

A key moment in thinking about this occurred for me as I was reading C.S. Lewis's *Prince Caspian*. As I read the following passage, I felt as if a light bulb had been switched on in my mind. It is an encounter between Lucy, one of the four children who have returned to the land of Narnia, and Aslan, the great lion. Lucy awakes from a deep sleep and is compelled to get up by the sound of a voice calling her name. She follows and shortly encounters Aslan himself.

> 'Aslan,' said Lucy, 'you're bigger.'
>> 'That is because you are older, little one,' answered he.
>> 'Not because you are?'
>> 'I am not. But every year you grow, you will find me bigger.'[3]

By contrast, according to Peter Brierley's research, young people in UK churches were not finding God to be bigger every year they grew; they were finding him smaller. A church's children's ministry may serve children well but fail to demonstrate God's presence, activity and relevance as those young people leave childhood behind.

As mentors, walking alongside young people, our role is to help them see that right where they currently are, God is present with them and is at work in them by his Spirit. We need to help them grow in their relationship with God, to grow in faith, recognising that although as children they may have related to him as a friend, as they grow they will come to know him as Saviour and Lord. And they will learn that for every different situation we face, he is still there, totally relevant to our experiences and ready to meet with us.

For some young people who grew up in church and came to faith as children, the teenage years involve a questioning of the validity of their childhood faith. It's not unusual for them to come back from a Christian event saying that they have really met with God and have now become 'real' Christians. In fact, it's not the case that they were not real Christians before; it's simply that they came to faith in childhood, now they have started to grow up, and God is meeting them in a different way. The role we can play is to help young people mark those moments of growing in God, moments they can look back on and recognise as points when their experience of God entered a new realm.

It's important that we do this in the ordinary moments as well, helping young people to see how the Holy Spirit has been changing them, helping them with behaviour patterns or attitudes about various life issues. As Paul Fenton writes:

> It is important that the young in faith hear about your 'faith benchmarks', when God has been close to you or when your understanding of him has been enlarged. The telling of stories remains one of the most compelling means of passing on knowledge and experience, and we are all the more caught up in a

story when it's about someone we are close to. We must learn to tell our stories so that young people can identify when God is close to them. We will also be helping them to pass on their faith stories to future generations.[4]

Sharing in the story of doubts

A few months ago, a friend in her early 20s arrived at my door in floods of tears. I invited her in and, over the following hour, listened to her as she explained the cause of her distress. Building inside her for quite a long time had been a real sense of doubt about her faith. How did she know it was for real? Did she believe it simply because she'd been brought up in a Christian home? If she'd been born into a Muslim family, would she not have been equally convinced about Islam? Then came the final question: 'Do you have times when you wonder if God actually does exist?'

There we were, swimming about in a sea of doubts, with wave after wave still coming. These were doubts that she'd never felt able to express, even though they'd crossed her mind on a number of occasions. At the same time, they were doubts that, at some point, most of us have faced, yet we are rarely good at sharing those doubts for fear of how we will be judged. The reality is that we will never remove these questions but can only delay the asking. My friend had tried to silence them for years but they emerged anyway.

John Westerhoff, a leading thinker in faith development, suggests that there are four stages we go through before we arrive at a point of 'owned faith'. Each stage builds on the one before, just as the rings grow in a tree trunk. The third stage that he talks about is called 'searching faith'. This is a crucial time of asking questions, of holding up to scrutiny everything that we have learnt. Such a stage often occurs in the early teenage years, but if, for whatever reason, it does not happen then, you can be sure it will appear at a later time.

Having the opportunity to ask questions and express doubts is vitally important for all of us, but particularly for young people. They need to be assured that questions and doubts don't negate their faith, but are in fact an essential part of building a strong faith.

So how do we help young people with their doubts? I think Paul Fenton offers some helpful words on this issue:

> The greatest witness at such a time will not be your words or even your knowledge, although these may help. Your role will be to reveal how you have struggled, and continue to struggle, with such complexities yourself. The very fact that you are willing to grapple with such issues, yet your faith carries on growing as a result, will be a witness to the effectiveness of Christ in your life.[5]

Times of doubt are as much a part of even the strongest Christian's faith as are the times of complete certainty and trust. In fact, it's often the times of doubt that lead to the strongest growth. There's something about knowing that we've faced our questions head on, we've presented them to God and he has responded (not necessarily with the answer you'd anticipated) that gives us confidence to go on trusting and growing. Mike Yaconelli puts it far more eloquently than I can, reflecting on his experience of doubt:

> There Jesus was in the eye of the stormy waters, asking me to come to Him. His gentleness was only perceptible because of the roaring waters around me. Give me a Jesus who meets me in the rushing, crashing waves of my questions. Let me stand precariously close to the dark and menacing skies of doubt, so I can hear the fierce and gentle loving voice of my Jesus who drowns out my fears and stands just beyond my questions with open arms.[6]

As God's people, we are deceiving ourselves when we try to protect young people from questions and doubts. Stories of all kinds often make us wait for the happy ending, so why should the story of faith be different? What matters is that we learn to listen to what God is saying in those times and learn to depend on the sufficiency of his grace.

Sharing in the story of celebration

One of the things I love most is meeting up with those who were part of that original youth group where we started exploring mentoring. I love these occasions when we get to meet again, catching up on what they are doing, how life is going and so on, but it's never too long before we start reminiscing. I know without a doubt that very soon someone will say, 'Do you remember when...?' More often than not, the remembering will be about some celebration that we had, whether it was to celebrate Christmas, the end of Holiday Club when we had all worked together on the team, or something that a group member had achieved.

Throughout Exodus, Leviticus, Numbers and Deuteronomy, God reminds his people to celebrate the Passover, so that they and the generations to come would remember the way he had delivered them from slavery. In Exodus 34:22, he commands them to celebrate the two harvest festivals, again to remember God's provision for them. In Deuteronomy 16:13, he commands them to celebrate the Feast of Tabernacles, to remind them of the way God provided for their ancestors who wandered in the desert without a home. In all these festivals, the Israelites were encouraged to stop, step back and give thanks for God's provision, for his faithfulness and for his never-failing love.

This is a good pattern for us to adopt, because we are God's people too. It is so easy to overlook all kinds of opportunities to celebrate. As goals are reached or new challenges faced and achieved, there is a chance to celebrate. It can be as simple as bringing cake to the next mentoring session or, if the occasion calls for it, you might want to organise a big party. Celebrating is good; it helps us to recognise and give thanks to the one who makes all things possible. Celebrating significant moments with young people will put some great deposits into their memory banks, and, in the coming years when they've moved away from home, may well provide reminders of God's activity in their life and keep them close to him.

Sharing in the story of failure

Jane was a faithful member of our youth group, very active in her school's Christian Union and totally committed to mentoring teenagers younger than herself. She was one of those people who seem to exude joy automatically, and was completely confident in sharing her faith with her friends. However, after a completely out-of-character action, she thought all this was going to come to an end. One weekend she'd been to a party and got drunk, and had ended up in a compromising situation with a boy she knew. Immediately she felt incredibly guilty. She was convinced that God could never forgive her and that she'd have to give up all her Christian leadership roles.

It was a couple of weeks before she came to talk to me. She couldn't keep her experience to herself any longer and needed someone to know about it. We talked together about the nature of God's forgiveness and, having prayed with her, I encouraged her to go home and read some verses that we'd looked at together and pray on her own. As she was leaving, I asked her why it had taken her so long to come to talk to me. Why had she gone on carrying this burden of guilt? Her response shocked me. Her perception of me was that I was a very good person, that I always did the right thing: I think the word 'perfect' might even have been used.

Now, I'm guessing you don't need me to tell you that I'm not perfect – not by a long shot. But she had never seen me behave in a less than 'good' way. She'd never heard me talk about mistakes that I'd made, so she'd felt that she couldn't talk to me because I wouldn't understand what it was like to get things wrong. I learnt so much that day. I learnt first-hand that the young people I lead have to know not just about my successes but also about my failures. They need to know that there are times when I let God down so spectacularly that I wonder if I can get up again, that daily I have to come to him for forgiveness, and daily he provides it.

It's not just teenagers who have times when they fail and let God down – and they desperately need to know that. They also need to know that although some mistakes will leave their mark on us, they will never prove fatal for our relationship with God.

An ongoing story

Kenda Creasy Dean says that if young people are to have an ongoing faith, there are four things that they need: a God worthy of belief, a community to belong to, a role to play and a hope to hold on to. None of these is going to be achieved by a teenager on their own.[7] Obviously it is God alone who does the work of faith and he is very active in teenagers' lives, but it seems to me that he has designed us to share the journey with other travellers, and to share our stories along the way, in order to know him better. The mentor's role is crucial in helping teenagers navigate the path at such a significant time in their lives.

Part IV

Mentoring for leadership

10

Identifying young leaders

To build leaders, start early.

Anon

As a teenager, I was very shy and had never imagined myself as a leader at all. Every year in the church where I grew up, we held a Holiday Club for children from the surrounding villages. It had run for a number of years and I'd helped out at it a good few times. Then one year we hit a bit of a problem, as the guy who usually led the club had moved to a different part of the country and was no longer able to continue in the role. A new leader was needed, and I was completely stunned when the minister asked me and another teenager if we would take charge of the event. To be honest, I was scared silly. I did a pretty good imitation of Moses in the excuses department, and my friend was close behind. We both agreed to take on the role, however, and, looking back, I am now so grateful that someone spotted some leadership ability in me and gave me the opportunity to play that role. It was a crucial moment for me in growing as a leader.

Debunking the myths

Leaders are born, not made

The question of whether leaders are born or made has been debated for years, and, while there is no denying that some people are most definitely born with leadership ability (you only have to go into a nursery to see that), the answer is, of course, that leaders can be both born and made. In addition, one is not better than the other. Even natural leaders need to learn and grow in leadership, because simply relying on innate talent is not enough.

Research carried out by the Kellogg Foundation concluded that 'the capacity to lead is rooted in virtually any individual... leadership is no longer the province of the few, the privileged or even the merely ambitious. Every student has the potential to be an effective leader'.[1]

Some young people will have a natural ability to take charge, while some may have other leadership abilities: some are great at public speaking, some can organise for Britain, while others are brilliant at getting people on board with a project. As mentors, we need to be identifying and encouraging all of these abilities.

Some young people are just not cut out to be leaders

What image comes into your mind when you hear the word 'leader'? We all have a default image, which comes from our experience of leadership or beliefs about leadership, and this image will hugely affect how we look at others in terms of leadership. We can have very clear ideas about what we think leadership is meant to look like and, if young people don't match up to those ideas, we jump to the conclusion that they therefore mustn't be leaders.

If John Maxwell is right, however, and leadership at its most basic is about influence, then we all have the potential to be leaders. What we do in terms of leadership will be different depending on who we are. Research has shown that experiences we have during our formative years greatly influence what we go on to do. If young people are not exposed to leadership opportunity during their teenage years, it is less likely that they will get involved in leadership until much later in life, if at all.

John Maxwell also gives some helpful thoughts on what we can expect from those who don't seem to have natural leadership ability. His premise is that everyone has some kind of leadership ability, but some will have more than others. Some might score quite highly on a scale of leadership talent while others rate much less. He asserts that because leadership can be learnt, everyone has the potential to move further up the scale from where they are, not necessarily to the top but further than where they currently are. Mentoring can help young people reach that potential.

Leaders are a certain type of personality

It used to be thought that leaders had to have a certain personality type to succeed but, thankfully, today it is recognised that there is more than one type of leader. Leadership is not merely the domain of the charismatic extravert; it's open to introverts, too. In fact, research has shown that the most effective leadership comes not from people whom we would label 'charismatic', but those who are 'inspirational'. What's the difference? A useful illustration is a comparison between Hitler and Churchill. Apparently, if you had an interview with Hitler, you left his presence thinking, 'That man can do anything.' If you had an interview with Churchill, however, you left his presence thinking, 'I can do anything.' That's the difference between charismatic and inspirational leadership. Both are effective leadership types (although you may want to argue that Hitler's leadership skills weren't put to good use), and are found in very different types of people.

What to look for in potential leaders

Taking on board the fact that more young people have leadership potential than we may initially think, but recognising the principle 'For the sake of the many, invest in a few', how do we identify who those 'few' should be?

It's interesting that when Jesus was faced with this situation, 'he went to a mountain to pray, and he prayed to God all night. At daybreak he called together all of his disciples and chose twelve of them to be apostles' (Luke 6:12–13). We should remember that on the day when

Jesus called the Twelve, it was not the first time he'd met them. Up to this point, he'd been travelling around with a crowd of people, but he knew that if he was to develop the future leaders of the Church, he needed to focus on a few of them. So what was it about these twelve that meant they were chosen? Had they proven themselves more capable or dependable than the rest? Were they more fun to be with? Did they have greater wisdom than the others? The truth is that we don't know. All we do know is that before making his choice, Jesus spent the night in conversation with his Father.

That's the right starting point for us, too. If we want to remove the blinkers from our eyes that prevent us from seeing certain types of people as leaders, then this can best happen in conversation with our heavenly Father. We need to take time to ask him to bring to our minds those whom he is calling.

Prayer must be our priority when looking for young leaders, but there are some other indicators that we can look for in young people, which might suggest that they are ready to be mentored in leadership.

Every year we used to run a youth Alpha course with our youth group, to which they would invite their friends. After the first course, though, we invited different young people to take on the role of small group leaders. It created an interesting dynamic when some were not asked, who thought they should have been. A number came to speak to me about why they had been overlooked, and it provided an excellent opportunity to explain to them what we were looking for in terms of potential leaders. Some then rose to the challenge, got serious about working on their character and, the following year, took up the roles that they hadn't been ready for just twelve months earlier.

The following five characteristics were the qualities that I told them I was looking for:

Commitment to spiritual growth

If we're looking for someone to develop in Christian leadership, their first priority must be their commitment to growing spiritually. Many young people are keen to get involved with the stuff upfront, in the spotlight. Fewer are prepared to put in the discipline behind the scenes, to grow in their relationship with God. As I look for those to develop, I'm most certainly not looking for perfection but I am looking for those who show evidence of the fruit of the Spirit in their lives.

Courage

Leadership requires courage – courage to say 'yes' to certain things and courage to say 'no', even if it involves going against the flow. How does courage manifest itself in young people? It does so in a number of ways. Firstly, it's shown in those who are willing to share their opinions openly. Many young people keep quiet, even if they have a strong opinion about something or are certain that they know the right answer, for fear of making a mistake or of what their peers might think. Young people with courage may be concerned about the same issues but they are prepared to take a risk because they want to be fully involved in those issues.

Courage is also shown by those who are willing to stand up for what they believe, or on behalf of others in difficult circumstances. I think it's also seen in those who are willing to try something new, even if it takes them out of their comfort zone. As the saying goes, 'Courage isn't the absence of fear; it's facing the fear and doing it anyway.' If young people are to grow in their leadership skills, they must be ready to take a step beyond the place where they currently are, and they need courage for that.

People skills

Leadership is about leading people, so initially I look for those around whom others naturally congregate. I should sound a note of caution here, however, about mistaking popularity for leadership skill. Popularity has to be backed up with good character.

Secondly, I look for those who take the time to care for others. Jo is someone who instantly springs to mind. Every Thursday evening when our youth group met, Jo would spend most of the evening going round the group, chatting to each person individually, asking how their week has been and encouraging them in whatever they've been doing. She would spot those who were on the edge of the activities and had a brilliant way of getting them involved. Now Jo would never push herself forward as a leader – in fact, she's quite shy – but she most definitely has leadership skill.

Enthusiasm

Some people have a way of making anything look like fun, and their enthusiasm is so catching that before long others want to be involved. I look for those who willingly respond to activities, who get wholeheartedly on board with what's going on and enter fully into whatever is asked of them.

Willingness to serve

A wise person once told me that a large part of Christian ministry is about putting out chairs. So far in my experience, he has been proved right. At its heart, Christian leadership is about servanthood. Jesus made it very clear that leadership in the kingdom of God turns on its head the leadership style of the world:

> You know that in this world kings are tyrants, and officials lord it over the people beneath them. But among you it should be quite different. Whoever wants to be a leader among you must be your

servant, and whoever wants to be first must be slave of all. For even I, the Son of Man, came here not to be served but to serve others, and to give my life as a ransom for many.

MARK 10:42–45

I look for those who turn up to help, those who are willing to stay behind after events to clear up, those who forgo time chatting with friends to wash up. These are the signs that someone has understood that leadership is about so much more than being out at the front.

This is by no means an exhaustive list, but if these five key characteristics are in place, at least in some measure, and the young person has a willingness to learn, you have a very solid foundation on which to build.

11

Created with purpose

The research company Gallup has done a lot of study in the area of leadership talent.[2] It has discovered that for good leadership to occur, 20 different leadership talents are required. Gallup's research shows, however, that no one person possesses all 20 talents. The most gifted of leaders will have, at most, somewhere between ten and 13 of them, which indicates that leadership happens best within a team context. What the research also uncovered (which interests me most) is the fact that our talents are formed in us by the time we reach our late teens.

That's quite sobering news for those of us of more mature years, who long to develop new areas of leadership talent, but it's good news for teenagers who still have the ability to do so. Although this research applies to all types of talent and not just talent for leadership, there is much that we can learn about the importance of working with people in their teenage years to develop them in leadership. This is the key time to invest in them, while their brains are still able to engage in the formation of new talent.

It might be worth taking a moment to look at how we define talent. The technical definition goes something like this: 'Talent is any recurring pattern of thought, feeling or behaviour that can be productively applied.'[3] The simpler version says, 'Talent is not what you can do; it's what you can't help yourself doing.'[4]

The brain is unusual in that whereas most organs in our body start small and grow along with us, the brain does the opposite: it gets big very quickly and shrinks as we grow older. Often, children are described as being like sponges, and that's a very accurate description as they are constantly soaking up everything around them and their brains are making links between everything that they experience. Many networks are developing between different parts of the brain, which help children to increase in skill. As we get older, the links that aren't used regularly fall into disrepair and we no longer have access to them. By the time we are 16, half of our networks will have fallen into disrepair.

For example, I studied French and Spanish for many years. I was fluent in both languages and could communicate happily and easily in them. In recent years I've not been back to France or Spain, and there is nobody nearby with whom I can talk in these languages on a regular basis. Now, when I want to speak either language, it feels as if there is too much that I just can't access in my brain: it's been filed away under 'non-current', allowing more frequently used skills to come to the fore.

It is extremely difficult for adults to create any new networks; childhood and the teenage years are the time for that to happen. If we want to grow strong leadership in adults, then, we need to start when they are young. Waiting until people are in their 20s and 30s to do it is just too late. The way to keep the leadership talent networks in our brain active is to use them frequently during the formative years and to continue doing so.

Who do you want to be?

Having said all that, let's not fall prey to the lie that the world is communicating to young people today – that they can be whoever they want to be and do whatever they want to do. They can't. There are some things in which, no matter how hard they try, a particular individual will never excel – because he or she has not been created in that way. We're not robots who can be programmed to carry out any task; we are lovingly created children of God. So, although young people can't be absolutely anything they want to be, they can be all that they've been created to be.

As mentors, we need to take every opportunity to help them discover what their leadership talents and gifts are. A good starting point is to help them think through the way God has uniquely created them. A tool that we've found useful in working with both adults and young people is the word 'SHAPE', which enables us to look at the different characteristics that are evident in our lives, to create a bigger picture of who we are and the leadership gifts and skills that we have. This model was developed by Rick Warren at Saddleback Church in America, and is explained in the book *S.H.A.P.E.* by Erik Rees (Zondervan, 2006).

- **S** stands for 'Spiritual gifts': the special gifts that God has given to his people.
- **H** stands for 'Heart': the things that we care deeply about.
- **A** stands for 'Abilities': the natural talents that we have.
- **P** stands for 'Personality': the way in which we are 'wired'.
- **E** stands for 'Experience': the collection of stuff from our past that God wants to use for others' futures.

Working through this word as you mentor a young leader will help them discover more about who God has created them to be, and how they can best serve him.

Spiritual gifts

This is what the Bible says about spiritual gifts:

God has given gifts to each of you from his great variety of spiritual gifts. Manage them well so that God's generosity can flow through you. Are you called to be a speaker? Then speak as though God himself were speaking through you. Are you called to help others? Do it with all the strength and energy that God supplies.

1 PETER 4:10–11

Spiritual gifts are gifts that God gives to his people to help the Church become all that it is meant to be. He doesn't give them so that people can feel proud of themselves, or to be, as my friend puts it, 'trophies for the mantelpiece'. Rather, he gives them as tools for the job of building the body of the Church so that we may witness in the world. The main biblical passages that identify the spiritual gifts are Romans 12:6–8; 1 Corinthians 12:8–10, 28 and Ephesians 4:11.

The difference between spiritual gifts and natural 'talents' is that the former are given by God to Christians for a specific purpose, and always to be used for the sake of the Church.

Some young people may already be aware of the spiritual gifts that God has given them, but many will not be sure what their gifts are. There are several tools available to help people discern their spiritual gifts, and you may want to consider working with one of these over a period of time. Alternatively, you may want to read the relevant Bible passages together, talking about what each gift means and identifying those that your mentoree has and those that they would like to develop.

One of the spiritual gifts is the gift of leadership, and in Romans 12:8 Paul exhorts us that, if leadership is our gift, we should lead with 'all diligence'. Presumably, if your mentoree has been identified as having leadership potential, this is one of the spiritual gifts that they will have been given. Thinking through the way that gift expresses itself in their life, and talking about what kind of leadership they would like to be involved in, will be well worth doing.

Heart

I recently reread the autobiography of Kay Warren (wife of Rick).[5] Kay describes herself as an average American woman who had spent most of her life getting on with the business of family life – until one morning in 2002.

The day had started like any other and, finding herself with some time to spare, Kay picked up a magazine from her coffee table. As she flicked through the magazine, her eye was caught by an article on AIDS orphans in Africa. This was not a new subject to her, as she'd been aware for years about the AIDS pandemic, yet on this morning it was as if she was reading about it for the first time. Her heart broke as she read about the twelve million children orphaned because of the disease, and her life has never been the same since. She found that she couldn't simply return the magazine to the table and get on with life as normal. The issue had taken hold of her heart and she knew that she had to do something about it. Today she splits her time between visiting places that are ravaged by HIV/Aids, offering support and teaching around the world on the subject, encouraging others to see the part they can play in alleviating this devastating disease.

I have a friend who, on a short-term mission trip to Thailand, was so appalled by the conditions there under which children with disabilities had to live, abandoned and rejected and with no hope of reaching their potential, that she changed the whole direction of her life. Nicola came back to the UK, researched different programmes and then returned to Thailand to set up a development project called '1 Step, 2 Step' for children with cerebral palsy. The situation had taken hold of her heart and she had to do something about it.

Because we have been created by God, he has left clues inside us about how he wants to use us. For each of us, the issue that takes hold of our hearts will be different, but God asks us to listen to our hearts and to respond to the nudges that we feel.

Here are some useful questions to ask, to help your mentoree think through the issues that they are passionate about:

- What are the areas in life where you would love to make a difference?
- If you could do anything at all, and it was guaranteed to succeed and your friends and family fully supported you in it, what would you do?
- What are the issues in your school, town, country or world that make you so exasperated that you feel you have to take action?

If your mentoree is not sure how to answer these questions, assure them that they don't need to worry. Now is the right time for them to be discovering the issues that God is putting on their heart to make a difference, areas in which he would like them to take a lead.

Abilities

I'm told that I didn't speak until I was quite old in developmental terms. Then, one day, I opened my mouth and started to speak pretty much perfectly. My friends and family will tell you that, since that moment, I haven't really stopped! Today, quite a large part of my job revolves around that ability. Singing is a different matter, however. One of my most humiliating moments at primary school was when I auditioned for the school choir. I was the only child who auditioned who didn't get in. To make matters worse, singing was one of my sister's greatest talents. I was devastated.

Some young people will be able to tell you immediately what they think their abilities are, but there are many teenagers who are convinced that they don't have any at all. As we mentor them, we can take time to help them work out what their abilities are.

Here are some questions that might help:

- What are the things that you love doing, that come fairly naturally and easily to you?
- Do you love to be out on the sports field?
- Do you enjoy being creative, either in thought or design?
- Are you musically talented?
- Do maths problems fill you with delight?
- Are you good at organising and do you thrive on it?
- Do you have the knack for motivating the people around you?
- Do you think nothing of cooking for 20 people?

These are all natural abilities. God's intention is that we link these abilities with our spiritual gifts and be inspired by our passion to do something that demonstrates his creativity and goodness to the world around us. It will be encouraging to think through all this with your mentoree, helping them see that God is involved in their lives and wants to use them to bring about the purposes of his kingdom.

Personality

There is no such thing as a good personality or a bad personality. We can be people of good or bad character, but personality is a different matter. Our character is something that, with God's help, we can work at changing, but our personalities are pretty much fully formed by the time we're four or five years old.

While our passions will help us work out where we might use our spiritual gifts and abilities, understanding our personality will go a long way to helping us work out how we will use our gifts and abilities. Our personalities affect the way in which we do everything, from making decisions, handling difficult situations and approaching new people down to whether we're more likely to approach something competitively or cooperatively.

Today there are many different tests that we can do to find out our personality type. Although they are helpful to a certain degree, they can sometimes end up putting us in boxes or providing us with good excuses for bad behaviour. 'That's just the way I am' is a well-worn phrase for explaining away our faults. However, there are some important truths that they can teach young people about themselves, from the way they respond to people and to different opportunities, which will give them a clue to the context in which their leadership will develop.

Some people are very outgoing and love to be surrounded by a crowd. Others prefer to have a few close friends. Some love being the centre of attention, while others are far happier behind the scenes. Some people love working with others, while others see everything as a competition. Some people will share anything and everything about their lives – how they're feeling, what's upsetting them, and so on – whereas others keep far more to themselves.

Young people need to know that being one way is not better than being another way. We're just different – and that's good news! If we were all out-and-out extroverts, constantly wanting the limelight, lots of people would feel overlooked. What is important is that we recognise how we're made so that we can look for opportunities suited to our personality. That doesn't mean we refuse to step out of our comfort zone every now and then, but it does mean that we know where we work best.

Experience

The final element that makes up our 'SHAPE' is our experiences, both good ones and bad. The person we are today has been moulded by the experiences that we've been through. Sometimes it's hard to understand how the difficulties we've experienced can ever be used for good, but they can. I'm amazed to see how often God brings people across my path who are going through something that I've experienced. At those times, I'm able to come alongside them, empathise with them and encourage them that their situation will get better.

Sensitively helping young people to think through their experiences at their own pace can help them make sense of what has happened to them, and enable them to see how God will use all things for good, as Paul writes to the church in Rome (see Romans 8:28).

In working through each of the five 'SHAPE' areas, the mentorees should start to see more clearly how God has shaped them, and should be encouraged about the leadership gifts and skills that he has given them. They will see more and more clearly what role they have to play today, using those gifts and skills to help lead his people and reach out to those who don't yet know him.

However, our aim should not be to give young people a completed, closed picture of who they are. Whereas, with adults, we would want to focus on one or two specific skills that they have, with teenagers we need to be giving them lots of opportunities to explore a whole range of possible areas where they might have leadership talent.

This means that young people must be given genuine opportunities to lead. The only way to develop gifts and skills is to use them. As mentors, we need to be helping young people to find meaningful ways of exercising their gifts and skills both inside and outside the church. Let's be people who open doors for the next generation, who give them opportunities to discover their talents and abilities and encourage them to step up and lead.

Edwin Meese, former attorney general of the USA, writes, 'In order to realise their leadership potential, young people need mentors who will give them responsibility and allow them to lead. That means they will make mistakes. That's to be expected – it's part of the learning process.'[6]

12

Not too heavy a load

One's mind, once stretched by a new idea, never regains its original dimensions.

Oliver Wendell Holmes

A number of years ago, when I was part of a church staff team, we carried out a survey about leadership. One of the questions was included to try to discover why people were reluctant to get involved in leadership. The responses fell mainly into two categories: first, there were people who had tried leading before and had felt abandoned in the role; second, there were those who had had an experience of leadership when they were younger but they had felt so out of their depth that they got out as soon as they could, and really didn't want to return to that kind of experience.

This flags up two warnings that we must heed as we mentor young people in leadership. We need to provide young people with appropriate and growing experiences of leadership, but without any sense of being 'dropped in at the deep end', beyond where they can manage to swim. If we manage their experience appropriately, situations that once represented the 'deep end' to them soon become comfortable swimming waters, and a new deep end will be revealed.

That's not to say that we don't put young people in challenging situations. I have discovered that when we raise the bar of our expectations, young people will often meet it and even go beyond it, but we must remember their age and their stage. They are not yet adults, and we must not lay on them a burden that is too heavy for them to carry. We must also make it clear that we are not expecting perfection from them and that it is okay if things don't go according to plan. If mistakes happen, our job is to help them recover from any sense of failure, as we have already seen.

Godly young leaders

As we come to a close, let's take a final moment to think ahead, to consider what the future could look like for the young people we know and for the lives of our churches.

Let's imagine what it would be like if our young people were growing in Christlike character, equipped to lead well in their churches, in their schools and colleges, and in their homes.

Let's imagine young leaders growing with an attitude of servant-hood, wherever they find themselves, using the abilities God has given them to lead others in ways that demonstrate God's love and achieve God's kingdom purposes.

Let's imagine young people confident in their place and their role in the kingdom of God today, encouraged to embrace everything that those roles demand of them.

Perhaps we can see the future in someone like Jo, mentioned earlier, whose leadership ability is most definitely expressed through her gift of encouragement.

Then there is Tim, who has recently started leading worship in the evening service, writing his own songs and really enjoying using his musical gifts to lead others.

Look at Jane, who is thinking about how she can show leadership at home and, as a result, is having an impact on her parents and her sister, prompting them to ask for themselves what it means to follow God.

Think of Edd, who chooses to demonstrate his servant-leadership as captain of the school hockey team. Having led his team in victory, he returns to the club house with players and parents, and is the first to take round the sandwiches, making sure that everyone has something to eat.

The picture that the Bible offers of the church is the image of a body. As each person, regardless of their age, is equipped for the works of service that God has prepared for them to do, the body of the church grows into full maturity, just as God intended.

For the sake of many, invest in a few

Mentoring young leaders really does have the potential to change a generation and renew leadership in both the church and the nation. My prayer is that as you embark on or continue with this amazing adventure, walking alongside young leaders at a most vital time in their lives, you would see God do far more than you could ever ask or imagine. As you invest in a few, and they go on to invest in a few more, his kingdom will come and lives will be transformed.

Appendix:
A plan for meeting

Introduction

There are four main objectives for the first meeting:

1 To start to establish the relationship between you and your mentoree.
2 To identify whether you both want to proceed with the mentoring relationship.
3 To form an agreement between you as the basis of your mentoring relationship.
4 To plan the dates of your next three meetings.

Some mentors will already know their mentoree, in which case they can probably move straight on to objectives 3 and 4. Others will be meeting for the first time and will need to take more time over objectives 1 and 2.

Objective 1: getting to know one another

The initial meeting is an opportunity to get to know one another, to pray together and decide whether or not you both want to continue. These questions could help:

- Tell me about yourself (general background, family history, what motivates you, interests, hobbies, strengths, gifts, 'growing edges').
- Tell me about your relationship with God (how it really is, not how it ought to be).

- Tell me about your leadership roles. (What is your vision? What enthuses you? Where are the challenges? How are you feeling about leadership?)
- Tell me about your hopes for this mentoring relationship.

Objective 2: deciding whether to continue

This decision may be made in the course of the meeting or it may be made with further thought after the meeting. It is vital that both parties feel able to say 'no' without any aspersions being cast on the other person.

Objective 3: forming an agreement

This is an informal agreement between the two of you, regarding how you will operate. Central to this agreement are your expectations of one another. Here are some areas you might like to clarify.

Clear expectations
- What does the mentoree think they are here to do?
- What role does the mentoree want the mentor to play?

Clear commitment
- It takes time for the relationship to be established, so no one should expect too much too soon.
- Both mentor and mentoree are expected to be committed to the relationship: keeping appointments and doing what is agreed between meetings will both be priorities.

Clear communication
- How are you going to communicate with one another?
- What level of confidentiality are you going to work with? (Please refer to chapter 5, on safeguarding, for more guidance on this.)
- What will accountability mean in this relationship?

Clear demarcation
- How often will you meet (once a fortnight/month, every six weeks), and for how long (between one hour and two)?
- What sort of contact, if any, will you have between meetings? Email? Text? (Again, please refer to chapter 5 on safeguarding.)

Clear evaluation
- How is the mentoring relationship going?
- Talk through the relationship from time to time (see page 120 for ideas on questions to ask).
- Modify your agreement to fit the real-life mentoring situation.

Clear end
- If and when the mentoring relationship ends, it should end well, not just fizzle out.
- Give thanks for all that has been good.
- Review what you've gained from the relationship.

Objective 4: set dates of meetings

If you agree to go ahead, ensure that you have at least the next three dates in the diary. Then, each time you meet, add in the next one. Meetings should take place approximately once a month.

Questions for ongoing sessions

Making the connection

Seek to discover the young person's present area of need and begin there. Goals for action set at the previous session may need to be put to one side or dealt with later if a pressing concern emerges.

- How are you? How are you doing?
- How are you really? (Ask this follow-up question if you detect a problem in the way they respond to the first.)

- How are you feeling?
- Do you want to talk about it? (Don't assume that they do.)

Reporting back

- How did you get on with the goals we set last time?
- What can we celebrate?
- What have you been able to accomplish?
- What are you finding difficult? How does that make you feel?
- Why do you think that is so?
- What help do you think you may need?

Development of spiritual life

- How are things with you and God? How does that make you feel?
- What experiences of prayer and meditation have you had this week?
- What difficulties or frustrations did you encounter?
- What are you doing to improve your knowledge, skills and personal and spiritual development?

Other aspects of personal life

- How are your friendships going?
- How are you maintaining your friendships?
- Tell me about your other relationships.
- How are things at home?
- In what ways will our discussions affect your family relationships and friendships?
- What has brought you joy and hope?
- What do you do for relaxation?

Reflection on leadership

- How is your leadership going? How do you feel about that?
- What brings you joy?

- What is of special concern to you?
- What is your greatest challenge? What are you doing to meet it?
- Where are you meeting opposition and how does that make you feel? How are you dealing with it?
- What are you doing to develop relationships with your contacts who are not yet Christians?
- In what ways do you show concern for people who are on the margins or excluded in your community?

Thinking through issues together

- What did you find helpful/unhelpful in…? How do you feel about it?
- Why do you think that was so?
- What would you do differently, and how?
- What do you think Jesus would do in a similar situation?
- Where does God fit in here?
- What does the Bible have to say on this?
- What do you think you could do about …? What are you basing that opinion on?
- What are your options? (Brainstorm if necessary.)
- Which option seems the most appropriate?
- How do you think that option will help you? (Ask this question particularly if you worry that it may not be helpful.)

Making an action plan

Explore all possible angles to the solutions of any problem, evaluating and prioritising them. Ask the young person to think about the solutions at the top of the list. Pray together during this time to try to discern what the Lord is saying.

- What could you work on between now and our next meeting? (Limit the number of tasks: if they have too many, help them to prioritise. Ask them to write out the tasks and make a copy for you.)

- What do you think might prevent you from doing what you want? How can you deal with this?
- What or whom do you think could help with this?
- Do you know a person whom you respect and trust, who may help to make this happen? What else might be of help?

Praying it through

- Whom could you ask to pray for you or with you about what we have discussed?
- Is there a big challenge that you are facing at present, that I can pray about?

Appraising the relationship

After three meetings, and again after seven meetings, it is worth reviewing how the relationship is going. During meetings three and seven indicate that there will be time for appraisal when you next meet, so that the young person can reflect beforehand.

- How are you finding our times together?
- What are you finding most helpful? Why?
- What are you finding least helpful? Why?
- Are your initial expectations being met?
- Are there ways we could improve these times?

At the end of the day, it's up to you and your mentoree to decide the flow of your meetings and the combination of elements that you want to include (see the suggestions given in chapter 2). The key thing is that, as mentors, we look for the way God is at work in the young person we're mentoring. Then we do all we can to support that work by praying for them and with them, listening to them, asking good questions of them and agreeing with them realistic goals for their development.

Notes

Chapter 1: A biblical perspective

1   Matt Summerfield, *Infocus: Mentoring DVD* (Authentic).
2   Robert Clinton, quoted in Tim Elmore, *Mentoring: How to invest your life in others* (Kingdom Publishing House, 1995), p. 23.
3   Bo Boshers and Judson Poling, *The Be With Factor* (Zondervan, 2006), p. 19
4   Paul Fenton, *Someone to Lean On* (Scripture Union, 1998), p. 9.

Chapter 2: Models of mentoring

1   John Mallison, *Mentoring to Develop Disciples and Leaders* (Scripture Union Australia, 1998), p. 23.
2   Mallison, *Mentoring to Develop Disciples and Leaders*, p. 13.
3   Boshers and Poling, *The Be With Factor*, p. 49.
4   Richard Dunn, *Shaping the Spiritual Life of Students* (IVP, 2001).

Chapter 3: Benefits of mentoring

1   Sharon Daloz Parks, *Big Questions, Worthy Dreams* (Jossey Bass, 2000), p. 128.

Chapter 4: The changing world of adolescence

1   Kenda Creasy Dean, Assistant Professor of Youth, Church and Culture at Princeton Theological Seminary.
2   Mark Easton, '10 reasons to cheer our teenagers': **bbc.co.uk/blogs/ thereporters/markeaston/2008/07/10_reasons_to_cheer_our_ teenag.html**
3   Jennifer Waddle, '10 most common problems teens face in 2021': **parentology.com/10-most-common-problems-teens-face-in-2019**
4   Dunn, *Shaping the Spiritual Life of Students*, p. 32.
5   Dunn, *Shaping the Spiritual Life of Students*, p. 20.

Chapter 5: Creating a safe environment

1   Boshers and Poling, *The Be With Factor*.
2   Taken from The Church of England Safer Environment and Activities document, 2019.
3   Boshers and Poling, *The Be With Factor*, p. 83.

Chapter 6: Putting a mentoring scheme in place

1   Eugenia Price, quoted in Dr Ted W. Engstrom and Dr Ron Jenson, *The Making of a Mentor* (Authentic, 2005), p. 174.

Chapter 7: The characteristics of a mentor

1   Dr Wayne Cordeiro, Senior Pastor of New Hope Christian Fellowship, Honolulu, Hawaii.
2   Richard Foster, *Celebration of Discipline* (Hodder & Stoughton, 1998).
3   John Allan, 'One to one', *Youthwork* magazine, June 2004.
4   Engstrom and Jenson, *The Making of a Mentor*, p. 29.

Chapter 8: Key skills and tools for mentoring

1   Pat Williams, *Coaching Your Kids to Be Leaders* (Hodder & Stoughton, 2008).
2   Tim Elmore, *Mentoring* (Wesleyan Publishing House, 1995), pp. 70–71.

Chapter 9: Sharing the journey

1   Fenton, *Someone to Lean On*, p. 37.
2   Ivy Beckwith, *Postmodern Children's Ministry* (Zondervan, 2004), p. 95.
3   C.S. Lewis, *Prince Caspian* (Fontana, 1980), p. 124 (first published 1951).
4   Fenton, *Someone to Lean On*, p. 85.
5   Fenton, *Someone to Lean On*, p. 95.
6   Mike Yaconelli, *Messy Spirituality* (Hodder & Stoughton, 2001).
7   Kenda Creasy Dean, *Practicing Passion* (Eerdmans, 2006).

Chapter 10: Identifying young leaders

1   Alexander and Helen Astin, *Leadership Reconsidered: A Kellogg Report* (The W.K. Kellogg Foundation, 2000).

Chapter 11: Created with purpose

1   Daloz Parks, *Big Questions, Worthy Dreams*.
2   Explored in Marcus Buckingham and Donald O. Clifton, *Now, Discover Your Strengths* (Pocket Books, 2005).
3   Buckingham and Clifton, *Now, Discover Your Strengths*, p. 48.
4   James Lawrence, *Growing Leaders* (BRF, 2004), p. 25.
5   Kay Warren, *Dangerous Surrender* (Zondervan, 2007).
6   Edwin Meese, quoted in Williams, *Coaching Your Kids to Be Leaders*, p. 235.

Bibliography

Alexander and Helen Astin, *Leadership Reconsidered: A Kellogg Report* (The W.K. Kellogg Foundation, 2000)

Ivy Beckwith, *Postmodern Children's Ministry: Ministry to Children in the 21st-Century Church* (Zondervan, 2004)

Bo Boshers and Judson Poling, *The Be With Factor: Mentoring Students in Everyday Life* (Zondervan, 2006)

Richard R. Dunn, *Shaping the Spiritual Life of Students: A Guide for Youth Workers, Pastors, Teachers and Campus Ministers* (IVP, 2001)

Tim Elmore, *Mentoring* (Wesleyan Publishing House, 1995)

Dr Ted W. Engstrom and Dr Ron Jenson, *The Making of a Mentor: 9 Essential Characteristics of Influential Christian Leaders* (Authentic, 2005)

Paul Fenton, *Someone to Lean On: Accompanying Young People on the Journey of Faith* (Scripture Union, 1998)

Richard Foster, *Celebration of Discipline* (Hodder & Stoughton, 1980)

Larry Kreider, *Authentic Spiritual Mentoring: Nurturing Younger Believers toward Spiritual Maturity* (Regal, 2008)

Jon Langford, *Can We Have a Chat?* (Grove, 2006)

John Mallison, *Mentoring to Develop Disciples and Leaders* (Scripture Union Australia, 1998)

Sharon Daloz Parks, *Big Questions, Worthy Dreams: Mentoring Young Adults in Their Search for Meaning, Purpose and Faith* (Jossey Bass, 2000)

Dallas Willard, *The Spirit of the Disciplines: Understanding How God Changes Lives* (Harper San Francisco, 1991)

Walter C. Wright, *Mentoring: The Promise of Relational Leadership* (Paternoster, 2004)

Mike Yaconelli, *Messy Spirituality* (Hodder & Stoughton, 2001)

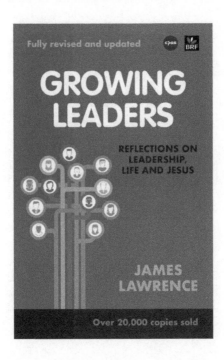

How do we keep growing as a leader? And how do we ensure others around us grow in their leadership? These twin themes run throughout this book, exploring the joys and challenges of leading at a time when we need Christians to lead well wherever they are. Such leadership is always about more than just skills. It includes a clearer sense of call, growth in Christlike character, an ability to lead well with others and, at heart, a deepening relationship with God. This book offer practical ideas and insights into how to grow as this sort of leader.

Growing Leaders
Reflections on leadership, life and Jesus
James Lawrence
978 0 85746 888 8 £10.99

brfonline.org.uk

Mentoring
Conversations
30 key topics to explore together

Tony Horsfall

A core resource for anyone involved in spiritual mentoring, *Mentoring Conversations* provides a basis for spiritual conversation in a mentoring context through 30 short chapters structured around six key topic areas: Foundations; Steps to growth; Living out your faith; Going deeper; Staying strong; and Living with mystery. Each chapter begins with a Bible passage or text, followed by the author's comment on the topic, questions for discussion, scriptures for further reflection and suggestions for further reading.

Mentoring Conversations
30 key topics to explore together
Tony Horsfall
978 0 85746 925 0 £9.99

brfonline.org.uk

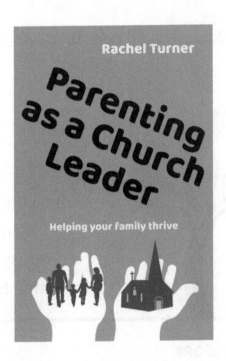

How do we spiritually parent our children while also needing to lead the church? How do we balance the many hats we wear? How do we live in a goldfish bowl and yet enable our children to flourish? How do we parent for faith without giving in to the pressure to perform for our congregations? Drawing on extensive research, this book explores the issues and builds a set of simple tools and approaches to help leaders and their families to flourish together.

Parenting as a Church Leader
Helping your family thrive
Rachel Turner
978 0 85746 937 3 £9.99

brfonline.org.uk

Enabling all ages to grow in faith

Anna Chaplaincy
Living Faith
Messy Church
Parenting for Faith

100 years of BRF

2022 is BRF's 100th anniversary! Look out for details of our special new centenary resources, a beautiful centenary rose and an online thanksgiving service that we hope you'll attend. This centenary year we're focusing on sharing the story of BRF, the story of the Bible – and we hope you'll share your stories of faith with us too.

Find out more at **brf.org.uk/centenary**.

To find out more about our work, visit

brf.org.uk